I0759710

A Midnight Treasury *of* *Macabre* *and* *Weird* *Poems*

Edited by
Ana Sampson

A Midnight Treasury *of* *Macabre* *and* *Weird* *Poems*

First published in 2025 by
Rizzoli Universe, a division of
Rizzoli International Publications

Rizzoli International Publications Inc
49 West 27th Street
New York, NY 10001

Rizzoli International Publications UK Ltd
Somerset House, West Wing
Strand, London WC2R 1LA

www.rizzoliusa.com

Publisher: Charles Miers
Associate Publisher: Tina Persaud
Designer: Steve Russell / aka-designaholic.com
Production Manager: Michelle Wells New
Senior Editor: Kristy Richardson

A CIP catalogue record for this book is available from the British Library.

ISBN 978-0-7893-4430-4

2025 / 1
Printed in China

The authorized representative in the EU for safety and compliance is Mondadori Libri S.p.A., via Gian Battista Vico 42, Milan, Italy, 20123, www.mondadori.it

Visit us online: Instagram.com/RizzoliBooks
Facebook.com/RizzoliNewYork
Youtube.com/user/RizzoliNY

Contents

Introduction

Welcome, traveller.

The night is wild and howling. By the ghastly light of a wan moon, things prowl among the trees and surge and slither in the breaking waves. Fear scuttles up your spine. Shapes best left half-seen rear up beside you, and you know – somehow, and suddenly – that you are something's prey. Branches clutch and claw. There are eyes everywhere. The path you had meant to take writhes like a snake. You are dizzy now, and far from home. You can no longer find yourself on any map.

You have heard the stories about this place, of course. Tales are whispered, warnings are hissed. You know, now, that there is no talisman that can steer you safely once you step across this threshold. You have stumbled, running widdershins, into the weird.

To enter the pages of this book is to stalk the streets of cities washed with blood, to sail unholy oceans and to roam uncanny forests – it is to know that you are not the first to pass this way. For hundreds of years, wild-eyed poets have sent us gothic dispatches from strange and cursed places, whether they found them in this world or within themselves. What an unsettling yet delicious pleasure it has been diving for these dark gems.

Within these covers, the time is out of joint and an unruly choir of voices sing out terrible tales. The hangman and the exorcist, the poisoner and the strangler are clamouring to tell you their stories – and you cannot cover your ears. There is William Blake – eyes ablaze – and wicked Lord Byron; Emily Dickinson, all in white, closeted in her house; and the Brontës keening on the moors. Here's Coleridge and sad wraith Lizzy Siddal, soused in laudanum, and the king of the macabre Edgar Allan Poe sweeping through with his retinue of ravens.

All the legions of Hell are gathered here. Monsters throng: dragons, the kraken, serpent women, the Jaberwocky. The Furies are abroad and their shadow falls darkly across you. No crime can go unpunished.

You might hear unearthly song ... is it a banshee or a siren, calling you with clear notes of terrible beauty? Entrust your heart to a demon lover, and you'll reap – as so many of these writers did – a vicious reward. There are goblins in the clearings and a changeling in the cradle. Who is to say the wolf is not your wife, or that your own hearth is a sanctuary? Everything here is eldritch; unfamiliar. The coven whirls you into their maddened moonlit dances – just don't ask who that horned figure is, watching over their revels. Tonight, the dead refuse to stay sleeping and rise up to hunt. They cannot be outrun.

You are pale, your teeth chattering between bloodless lips and eyes wide and haunted. What did you see out there? Did it chase you here?

As we learn from these strange meetings, 'foreheads of men have bled where no wounds were.' So it will take courage to turn these pages and step into these dark places. Do you dare, and will you be looking over your shoulder? The monster you fear the most may meet you in the mirror ...

Chapter One

Monsters Abroad *and* Within

"Their shrouds are bloody
and their lips are wet"

'Oil and Blood', W. B. Yeats

The World

By day she woos me, soft, exceeding fair:
But all night as the moon so changeth she;
Loathsome and foul with hideous leprosy,
And subtle serpents gliding in her hair.
By day she woos me to the outer air,
Ripe fruits, sweet flowers, and full satiety:
But thro' the night a beast she grins at me,
A very monster void of love and prayer.
By day she stands a lie: by night she stands
In all the naked horror of the truth,
With pushing horns and clawed and clutching hands.
Is this a friend indeed, that I should sell
My soul to her, give her my life and youth,
Till my feet, cloven too, take hold on hell?

Christina Rossetti

The Furies

Beneath the earth they wait   hissing
Deep in graves of dirt   listening
Blood-red eyes of hate   dripping

Each faithless man they take in turn
The violent husbands, liars, thieves
Ruled by lust, desire or greed
Are captured, never to return

With wings of bats unrolled   beating
Their skin is black as coal   glistening
Skulls with serpents coiled   shrieking

Torches, daggers, whips and knives
Teeming cups of poisoned drink
Nightmares issue from each wink
Justice is repaid with life

The vengeful sisters wait   unceasing
Administering their rage   believe it
So think before you play   or trick me

Lavinia Singer

Outlaws

Owls — they whinny down the night;
Bats go zigzag by.
Ambushed in shadow beyond sight
The outlaws lie.

Old gods, tamed to silence, there
In the wet woods they lurk,
Greedy of human stuff to snare
In nets of murk.

Look up, else your eye will drown
In a moving sea of black;
Between the tree-tops, upside down,
Goes the sky-track.

Look up, else your feet will stray
Towards that dim ambuscade
Where spider-like they catch their prey
In nets of shade.

For though creeds whirl away in dust,
Faith dies and men forget,
These agèd gods of fright and lust
Cling to life yet —

Old gods almost dead, malign,
Starving for unpaid dues:
Incense and fire, salt, blood and wine
And a drumming muse,

Banished to woods and a sickly moon,
Shrunk to mere bogey things,
Who spoke with thunder once at noon
To prostrate kings.

With thunder from an open sky
To warrior, virgin, priest,
Bowing in fear with a dazzled eye
Towards the dread East —

Proud gods, humbled, sunk so low,
Living with ghosts and ghouls,
And ghosts of ghosts and last year's snow
And dead toadstools.

Robert Graves

Skin

The men wore human skins
but removed them at night
and fell to the bottom of darkness
like crows without wings.

War was the perfect disguise.
Their mothers would not have known them,
and the swarming flies could not find them.

When they met a spirit in the forest
it thought they were bags of misfortune
and walked away
without taking their lives.

In this way, they tricked the deer.
It had wandered into the forest at night,
thinking antlers of trees
were other deer.

If I told you the deer was a hide of light
you wouldn't believe it, or that it was a hunting song
that walked out of a diviner's bag
sewn from human skin.

It knew it could pass
through the bodies of men and could return.
It knew the arrow belonged to the bow,
and that men only think they are following
the deaths of animals
or other men
when they are walking into the fire.

That's why fire is restless
and smoke has become
the escaped wings of crows,
why war is only another skin,
and hunting,
and why men are just the pulled-back curve of the bow.

Linda Hogan

Worm Interviewed

It said it was the resurrection's worm
Coiling its long whip in the empty vein;
Again, it said, I am the carnal worm
Sprung sweetly from the tissue of the head;
I, and I only, know the marrows of the brain,
The mysterious issue of the infertile egg.

I caused the mind-storm in the summer,
Throwing my long spear in the blood;
I caused the cracking of the missing rib,
My teeth the chisel and my eye the hammer.
Being the maggot in the newly dead
I heard the last pulse come bitterly.

I stole the tendon from the fractured foot
As scaffolding to bolster up my hollow nest;
I stole the nerve that held the eye to socket,
Now dropped aimlessly upon the cheek.
I was the asp about the virgin's breast
That made the milk to run at Christmastime.

I was the first thing and am last;
I made the bone that cowered in the womb,
My nest about it made the firm hard limb.
I am the Maker who does not count the cost
Of the long shelter of the shallow tomb.
I am the Priest who battens on the dead.

Ruthven Todd

The Mummy Invokes His Soul

Down to me quickly, down! I am such dust,
Baked, pressed together; let my flesh be fanned
With thy fresh breath; come from thy reedy land
Voiceful with birds; divert me, for I lust
To break, to crumble – prick with pores this crust! –
And fall apart, delicious, loosening sand.
Oh, joy, I feel thy breath, I feel thy hand
That searches for my heart, and trembles just
Where once it beat. How light thy touch, thy frame!
Surely thou perchest on the summer trees ...
And the garden that we loved? Soul, take thine ease,
I am content, so thou enjoy the same
Sweet terraces and founts, content, for thee,
To burn in this immense torpidity.

Michael Field

Appetit

Persephone meets her betrothed

Bet is to be wedded than to brynne
he said I was a peach

couldn't see him didn't know the crocus
pollen on my toes would be a dowry

black earth gulped my legs my shoulders
covered my head my footprints with itself

the taste of aquifers stone forests
mantle *I am dead* I reasoned

through dusted lashes knelt
somewhere head bowed   informed I am

to be comfort for a mud king
with strange pets

I gripped a grass blade still
bright with my own kissed breath

there was a wed-ing of sorts
my stomach and other parts   surveyed

to fathom my capacity
hung from my feet to siphon sunlight

blood pressed for foxglove poisons
panned for gold molecules

then began the drinking   a feast of carrion
the maltworm king crowed his huge

knowledge of human weakness *how fitting you are mine*
he cracked   *for the price of your hunger*

how fitting he   the corpse lord   mistook silence
for surrender and half-sober stirs

face down on his throne mound   bound
under my foot my heel in grey cheekflesh

and at my word forfeits all but
everything of his   even the dogs

Kit Byford

The Warning

Just now,
Out of the strange
Still dusk . . as strange, as still . .
A white moth flew. Why am I grown
So cold?

Adelaide Crapsey

Nightmare (extract from *The Botanic Garden*)

So on his Nightmare through the evening fog
Flits the squab Fiend o'er fen, and lake, and bog;
Seeks some love-wildered maid with sleep oppressed,
Alights, and grinning sits upon her breast.
—Such as of late amid the murky sky
Was marked by Fuseli's poetic eye,
Whose daring tints, with Shakespeare's happiest grace,
Gave to the airy phantom form and place.—
Back o'er her pillow sinks her blushing head,
Her snow-white limbs hang helpless from the bed,
While with quick sighs, and suffocative breath,
Her interrupted heart-pulse swims in death.
—Then shrieks of captured towns, and widows' tears,
Pale lovers stretched upon their blood-stained biers,
The headlong precipice that thwarts her flight,
The trackless desert, the cold starless night,
And stern-eyed murderer with his knife behind,
In dread succession agonize her mind.
O'er her fair limbs convulsive tremors fleet,
Start in her hands, and struggle in her feet;
In vain to scream with quivering lips she tries,
And strains in palsied lids her tremulous eyes;
In vain she *wills* to run, fly, swim, walk, creep;
The will presides not in the bower of Sleep.
—On her fair bosom sits the Demon-Ape
Erect, and balances his bloated shape;
Rolls in their marble orbs his Gorgon-eyes,
And drinks with leathern ears her tender cries.

Erasmus Darwin

The Beast

In our house he stalks silent
on padded feet. He has left
cracks on the floorboards, gouged
chasms in my father's face, ripped
bloody rivers across his eyes.
My mother believes she has
tamed him. Nights, she strokes his coarse
fur, coaxes him onto her
bed, his huge weight
rocks on her chest. Purring like thunder
shakes the curtains. In pitiful mucousy
scratching her breathing
aggravates the night. There are
bloodspots on her pillow. Hers.
He's been king in our house
for thirty years now. I told them
– Don't keep pets, they will
devour you. Leave them
roam the wide bush. He heard.
He knocked me to the ground
with a massive paw
flexed his claws on my back
licked the blood with his bone-cold
reptile tongue. I cowered on the floor
screaming. His great jaws
smiled over me, yellow black-flecked
teeth had bits of
raw meat in them. His breath came in hot
foul smelling waves. Don't
show fear, said my mother, he
likes you. – He
lives here, said my father, he's
one of us. You'll have to
get to know him. I saw his arm was
scarred with claw marks
wrist to shoulder.
– He's old, said my father, be
gentle with him.
You'll learn.

Jeni Couzyn

The Raven (extract)

Once upon a midnight dreary, while I pondered, weak and weary,
Over many a quaint and curious volume of forgotten lore—
While I nodded, nearly napping, suddenly there came a tapping,
As of some one gently rapping, rapping at my chamber door.
''Tis some visitor,' I muttered, 'tapping at my chamber door—
Only this and nothing more.'

Ah, distinctly I remember it was in the bleak December;
And each separate dying ember wrought its ghost upon the floor.
Eagerly I wished the morrow;—vainly I had sought to borrow
From my books surcease of sorrow—sorrow for the lost Lenore—
For the rare and radiant maiden whom the angels name Lenore—
Nameless *here* for evermore.

And the silken, sad, uncertain rustling of each purple curtain
Thrilled me—filled me with fantastic terrors never felt before;
So that now, to still the beating of my heart, I stood repeating
''Tis some visitor entreating entrance at my chamber door—
Some late visitor entreating entrance at my chamber door;—
This it is and nothing more.'

Open here I flung the shutter, when, with many a flirt and flutter,
In there stepped a stately Raven of the saintly days of yore;
Not the least obeisance made he; not a minute stopped or stayed he;
But, with mien of lord or lady, perched above my chamber door—
Perched upon a bust of Pallas just above my chamber door—
Perched, and sat, and nothing more.

'Prophet!' said I, 'thing of evil!—prophet still, if bird or devil!—
By that Heaven that bends above us—by that God we both adore—
Tell this soul with sorrow laden if, within the distant Aidenn,
It shall clasp a sainted maiden whom the angels name Lenore—
Clasp a rare and radiant maiden whom the angels name Lenore.'
Quoth the Raven, 'Nevermore.'

'Be that word our sign of parting, bird or fiend!,' I shrieked, upstarting—
'Get thee back into the tempest and the Night's Plutonian shore!
Leave no black plume as a token of that lie thy soul hath spoken!
Leave my loneliness unbroken!—quit the bust above my door!
Take thy beak from out my heart, and take thy form from off my door!'
    Quoth the Raven, 'Nevermore.'

And the Raven, never flitting, still is sitting, *still* is sitting
On the pallid bust of Pallas just above my chamber door;
And his eyes have all the seeming of a demon's that is dreaming,
And the lamp-light o'er him streaming throws his shadow on the floor;
And my soul from out that shadow that lies floating on the floor
    Shall be lifted—nevermore!

Edgar Allan Poe

The Twa Corbies

As I was walking all alane
I heard twa corbies making a mane;
The tane unto the t'other say,
'Where sall we gang and dine to-day?'

'–In behint yon auld fail dyke,
I wot there lies a new-slain knight;
And naebody kens that he lies there,
But his hawk, his hound, and his lady fair.

'His hound is to the hunting gane,
His hawk to fetch the wild-fowl hame,
His lady's ta'en another mate,
So we may mak our dinner sweet.

'Ye'll sit on his white hause-bane,
And I'll pick out his bonny blue een;
Wi' ae lock o' his gowden hair
We'll theek our nest when it grows bare.

'Mony a one for him makes mane,
But nane sall ken where he is gane;
O'er his white banes, when they are bare,
The wind sall blaw for evermair.'

Anonymous

Song

Old Adam, the carrion crow,
The old crow of Cairo;
He sat in the shower, and let it flow
Under his tail and over his crest;
And through every feather
Leaked the wet weather;
And the bough swung under his nest;
For his beak it was heavy with marrow.
Is that the wind dying? O no;
It's only two devils, that blow
Through a murderer's bones, to and fro,
In the ghosts' moonshine.

Ho! Eve, my gray carrion wife,
When we have supped on kings' marrow,
Where shall we drink and make merry our life?
Our nest it is queen Cleopatra's skull,
'Tis cloven and cracked,
And battered and hacked,
But with tears of blue eyes it is full:
Let us drink then, my raven of Cairo.
Is that the wind dying? O no;
It's only two devils, that blow
Through a murderer's bones, to and fro,
In the ghosts' moonshine.

Thomas Lovell Beddoes

The Demon of the Gibbet

There was no west, there was no east,
No star abroad for eyes to see;
And Norman spurred his jaded beast
Hard by the terrible gallows-tree.

"O, Norman, haste across this waste,—
For something seems to follow me!"
"Cheer up, dear Maud, for, thanked be God,
We nigh have passed the gallows-tree!"

He kissed her lip; then—spur and whip!
And fast they fled across the lea.
But vain the heel, the rowel steel,—
For something leaped from the gallows-tree!

"Give me your cloak, your knightly cloak,
That wrapped you oft beyond the sea!
The wind is bold, my bones are old,
And I am cold on the gallows-tree!"

"O holy God! O dearest Maud,
Quick, quick, some prayers—the best that be!
A bony hand my neck has spanned,
And tears my knightly cloak from me!"

"Give me your wine,—the red, red wine,
That in a flask hangs by your knee!
Ten summers burst on me accurst,
And I am athirst on the gallows-tree!"

"O Maud, my life, my loving wife!
Have you no prayer to set us free?
My belt unclasps,—a demon grasps,
And drags my wine-flask from my knee!"

"Give me your bride, your bonnie bride,
That left her nest with you to flee!
O she hath flown to be my own,
For I'm alone on the gallows-tree!"

"Cling closer, Maud, and trust in God!
Cling close!—Ah, heaven, she slips from me!"
A prayer, a groan, and he alone
Rode on that night from the gallows-tree.

Fitz-James O'Brien

The Hand of Glory: The Nurse's Story (extract)

There's a black gibbet frowns upon Tappington Moor,
Where a former black gibbet has frown'd before:
It is as black as black may be,
And murderers there
Are dangling in air,
By one!— by two!— by three!

There's a horrid old hag in a steeple-crown'd hat,
Round her neck they have tied to a hempen cravat
A Dead Man's hand, and a dead Tom Cat!
They have tied up her thumbs, they have tied up her toes,
They have tied up her eyes, they have tied up her limbs!
Into Tappington mill-dam souse she goes,
With a whoop and a halloo!—'She swims!— She swims!'
They have dragg'd her to land,
And every one's hand
Is grasping a faggot, a billet, or brand,
When a queer-looking horseman, drest all in black,
Snatches up that old harridan just like a sack
To the crupper behind him, puts spurs to his hack,
Makes a dash through the crowd, and is off in a crack!
No one can tell,
Though they guess pretty well,
Which way that grim rider and old woman go,
For all see he's a sort of infernal Ducrow;
And she scream'd so, and cried,
We may fairly decide
That the old woman did not much relish her ride!

R. H. Barham

I Saw a Chapel

I saw a chapel all of gold
That none did dare to enter in
And many weeping stood without
Weeping mourning worshipping

I saw a serpent rise between
The white pillars of the door
And he forcd & forcd & forcd
Down the golden hinges tore

And along the pavement sweet
Set with pearls and rubies bright
All his slimy length he drew
Till upon the altar white

Vomiting his poison out
On the bread & on the wine
So I turnd into a sty
And laid me down among the swine

William Blake

The Faerie Queene (extract)

But full of fire and greedy hardiment,
The youthfull knight could not for ought be staide,
But forth unto the darksome hole he went,
And lookèd in: his glistring armor made
A litle glooming light, much like a shade,
By which he saw the ugly monster plaine,
Halfe like a serpent horribly displaide,
But th' other halfe did womans shape retaine,
Most lothsom, filthie, foule, and full of vile disdaine.

And as she lay upon the durtie ground,
Her huge long taile her den all overspred,
Yet was in knots and many boughtes upwound,
Pointed with mortall sting. Of her there bred
A thousand yong ones, which she dayly fed,
Sucking upon her poisonous dugs, eachone
Of sundry shapes, yet all ill favorèd:
Soone as that uncouth light upon them shone,
Into her mouth they crept, and suddain all were gone.

Edmund Spenser

Paradise Lost (Book 10, extract)

His visage drawn he felt to sharp and spare,
His arms clung to his ribs, his legs entwining
Each other, till supplanted, down he fell
A monstrous serpent on his belly prone,
Reluctant, but in vain; a greater power
Now ruled him, punished in the shape he sinned,
According to his doom. He would have spoke,
But hiss for hiss returned with forkèd tongue
To forkèd tongue, for now were all transformed
Alike, to serpents all, as accessories
To his bold riot. Dreadful was the din
Of hissing through the hall, thick-swarming now
With complicated monsters head and tail—
Scorpion and asp, and amphisbaena dire,
Cerastes horned, hydrus, and ellops drear,
And dipsas (not so thick swarmed once the soil
Bedropped with blood of Gorgon, or the isle
Ophiusa); but still greatest he the midst,
Now dragon grown, larger than whom the sun
Engendered in the Pythian vale on slime,
Huge Python; and his power no less he seemed
Above the rest still to retain.

John Milton

Lamia (extract)

Left to herself, the serpent now began
To change; her elfin blood in madness ran,
Her mouth foam'd, and the grass, therewith besprent,
Wither'd at dew so sweet and virulent;
Her eyes in torture fix'd, and anguish drear,
Hot, glaz'd, and wide, with lid-lashes all sear,
Flash'd phosphor and sharp sparks, without one cooling tear.
The colors all inflam'd throughout her train,
She writh'd about, convuls'd with scarlet pain:
A deep volcanian yellow took the place
Of all her milder-moonèd body's grace;
And, as the lava ravishes the mead,
Spoilt all her silver mail, and golden brede;
Made gloom of all her frecklings, streaks and bars,
Eclips'd her crescents, and lick'd up her stars:
So that, in moments few, she was undrest
Of all her sapphires, greens, and amethyst,
And rubious-argent: of all these bereft,
Nothing but pain and ugliness were left.

John Keats

The Faerie Queene (extract)

By this the dreadfull Beast drew nigh to hand,
Halfe flying, and halfe footing in his hast,
That with his largenesse measurèd much land,
And made wide shadow under his huge wast,
As mountaine doth the valley overcast.
Approching nigh, he rearèd high afore
His body monstrous, horrible, and vaste,
Which to increase his wondrous greatnesse more,
Was swolne with wrath, and poyson, and with bloudy gore.

His huge long tayle wound up in hundred foldes,
Does overspred his long bras-scaly backe,
Whose wreathèd boughts when ever he unfoldes,
And thicke entangled knots adown does slacke,
Bespotted as with shields of red and blacke,
It sweepeth all the land behind him farre,
And of three furlongs does but litle lacke;
And at the point two stings in-fixèd arre,
Both deadly sharpe, that sharpest steele exceeden farre.

But stings and sharpest steele did far exceed
The sharpnesse of his cruell rending clawes;
Dead was it sure, as sure as death in deed,
What ever thing does touch his ravenous pawes,
Or what within his reach he ever drawes.
But his most hideous head my toung to tell
Does tremble: for his deepe devouring jawes
Wide gapèd, like the griesly mouth of hell,
Through which into his darke abisse all ravin fell.

And that more wondrous was, in either jaw
Three ranckes of yron teeth enraungèd were,
In which yet trickling blood and gobbets raw
Of late devourèd bodies did appeare,
That sight thereof bred cold congealèd feare:
Which to increase, and all at once to kill,
A cloud of smoothering smoke and sulphur seare
Out of his stinking gorge forth steemèd still,
That all the ayre about with smoke and stench did fill.

Edmund Spenser

Jabberwocky

'Twas brillig, and the slithy toves
Did gyre and gimble in the wabe:
All mimsy were the borogoves,
And the mome raths outgrabe.

'Beware the Jabberwock, my son!
The jaws that bite, the claws that catch!
Beware the Jubjub bird, and shun
The frumious Bandersnatch!"

He took his vorpal sword in hand:
Long time the manxome foe he sought—
So rested he by the Tumtum tree,
And stood awhile in thought.

And, as in uffish thought he stood,
The Jabberwock, with eyes of flame,
Came whiffling through the tulgey wood,
And burbled as it came!

One, two! One, two! And through and through
The vorpal blade went snicker-snack!
He left it dead, and with its head
He went galumphing back.

'And hast thou slain the Jabberwock?
Come to my arms, my beamish boy!
O frabjous day! Callooh! Callay!'
He chortled in his joy.

'Twas brillig, and the slithy toves
Did gyre and gimble in the wabe:
All mimsy were the borogoves,
And the mome raths outgrabe.

Lewis Carroll

Do You Hear Me, Mere-Watcher?
(Grendel's Mother calls out as Beowulf approaches the mere)

I'll suck sap your strength
til your muscular trunk clunks to dirt
and the beetles in your stink-black
heart scuttle out reeling

I'll sink incisors into your sword-grip
scratch and gash til my name
claws up your throat you retch up
untydre, waelgæst, aglæcwif

I'll give you female combat
and it isn't swordsong or wolfprowl

it's kite-shriek anger
red with mother-blood

nostril-flared, nail-pinched
silence, being mistaken, taken
for a meek-mild maiden

when with my *fyrwit* I'll burn your
mangy bone-house to claggy ash
hurl your *guð-grædig* daggers
into my mere where they'll rust
and rest and no one will dare
to look for them and I'll be glad
and I'll say so what

So fucking what?

Laura Varnam

untydre: evil progeny; *waelgæst*: slaughter-guest
aglæcwif: formidable female opponent
fyrwit: intelligence / curiosity (fire-wit)
guð-grædig: war-greedy

The Kraken

Below the thunders of the upper deep;
Far, far beneath in the abysmal sea,
His ancient, dreamless, uninvaded sleep
The Kraken sleepeth: faintest sunlights flee
About his shadowy sides: above him swell
Huge sponges of millennial growth and height;
And far away into the sickly light,
From many a wondrous grot and secret cell
Unnumbered and enormous polypi
Winnow with giant fins the slumbering green.
There hath he lain for ages and will lie
Battening upon huge sea worms in his sleep,
Until the latter fire shall heat the deep;
Then once by men and angels to be seen,
In roaring he shall rise and on the surface die.

Alfred, Lord Tennyson

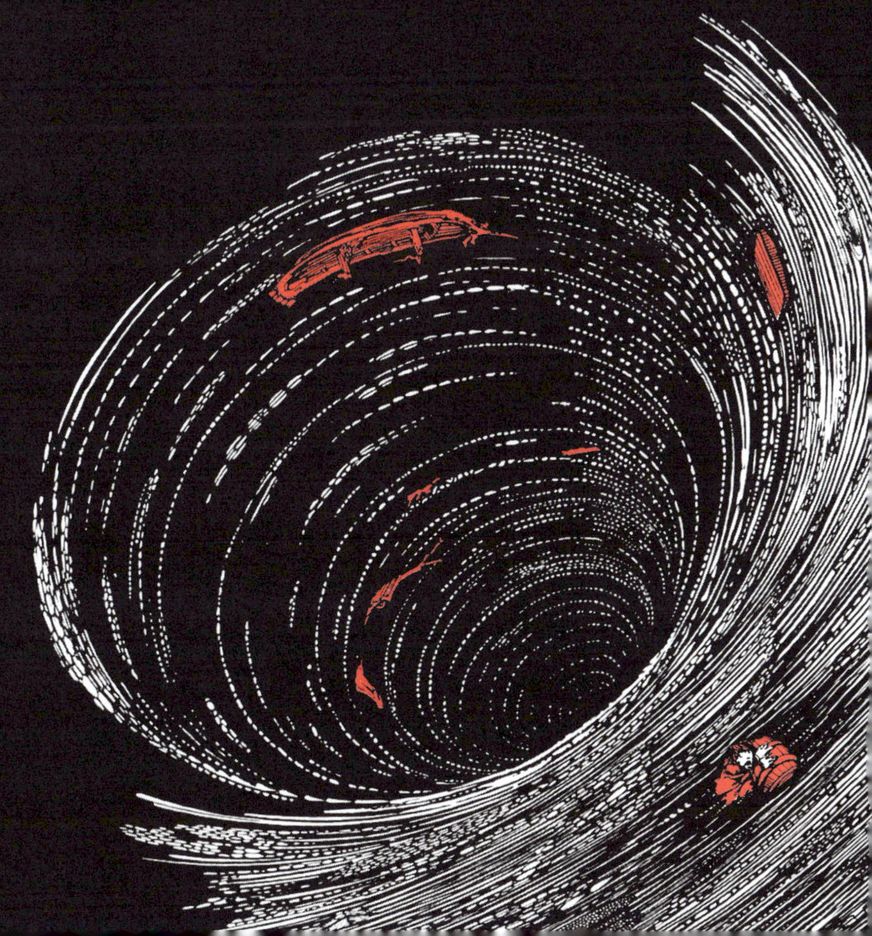

Will-O'-The-Wisp

I

There in the calamus he stands
With frog-webbed feet and bat-winged hands;
His glow-worm garb glints goblin-wise;
And elfishly, and elfishly,
Above the gleam of owlet eyes,
A death's-moth cap of downy dyes
Nods out at me, nods out at me.

II

Now in the reeds his face looks white
As witch-down on a witches' night;
Now through the dark old haunted mill,
So eerily, so eerily,
He flits; and with a whippoorwill
Mouth calls, and seems to syllable,
"Come follow me! come follow me!"

III

Now o'er the sluggish stream he wends,
A slim light at his finger-ends;
The spotted spawn, the toad hath clomb,
Slips oozily, slips oozily;
His easy footsteps seem to come –
Like bubble-gaspings of the scum –
Now near to me, now near to me.

IV

There by the stagnant pool he stands,
A fox-fire lamp in flickering hands;
The weeds are slimy to the tread,
And mockingly, and mockingly,
With slanted eyes and eldritch head
He leans above a face long dead, –
The face of me! the face of me!

Madison Cawein

Ginny Green Teeth

Ginny Green Teeth is hiding in the water,
Ginny Green Teeth is the Devil's own daughter.

Out among the shallows of the boggy Cheshire plain,
underneath the duckweed, there's a demon that's a-laying,
waiting for a wanderer to step too close and then
they're pulled into the underworld and never seen again.

Ginny Green Teeth is hiding in the water,
Ginny Green Teeth is the Devil's own daughter.

Children of the villages are warned to never play
anywhere near marshy ground or swampy waterway.
When moonlight on the sniddlebog is shining clear and cold,
the water-wench is prowling, on the hunt for careless souls.

Ginny Green Teeth is hiding in the water,
Ginny Green Teeth is the Devil's own daughter.

Matt Goodfellow

The Water-Nymph and the Boy

I flung me round him,
I drew him under;
I clung, I drown'd him,
My own white wonder! ...

Father and mother,
Weeping and wild,
Came to the forest,
Calling the child,
Came from the palace,
Down to the pool,
Calling my darling,
My beautiful!
Under the water,
Cold and so pale!
Could it be love made
Beauty to fail?

Ah me for mortals!
In a few moons,
If I had left him,
After some Junes
He would have faded,
Faded away,
He, the young monarch, whom
All would obey,
Fairer than day;
Alien to springtime,
Joyless and gray,
He would have faded,
Faded away,
Moving a mockery,
Scorn'd of the day!
Now I have taken him
All in his prime,
Saved from slow poisoning
Pitiless Time,
Fill'd with his happiness,

One with the prime,
Saved from the cruel
Dishonour of Time.
Laid him, my beautiful,
Laid him to rest,
Loving, adorable,
Softly to rest,
Here in my crystalline,
Here in my breast!

Roden Berkeley Wriothesley Noel

The Stolen Child

Where dips the rocky highland
Of Sleuth Wood in the lake,
There lies a leafy island
Where flapping herons wake
The drowsy water-rats;
There we've hid our faery vats,
Full of berries
And of reddest stolen cherries.
Come away, O human child!
To the waters and the wild
With a faery, hand in hand,
For the world's more full of weeping than you can understand.

Where the wave of moonlight glosses
The dim grey sands with light,
Far off by furthest Rosses
We foot it all the night,
Weaving olden dances,
Mingling hands and mingling glances
Till the moon has taken flight;
To and fro we leap
And chase the frothy bubbles,
While the world is full of troubles
And anxious in its sleep.
Come away, O human child!
To the waters and the wild
With a faery, hand in hand,
For the world's more full of weeping than you can understand.

Where the wandering water gushes
From the hills above Glen-Car,
In pools among the rushes
That scarce could bathe a star,
We seek for slumbering trout
And whispering in their ears
Give them unquiet dreams;
Leaning softly out
From ferns that drop their tears
Over the young streams.
Come away, O human child!
To the waters and the wild
With a faery, hand in hand,
For the world's more full of weeping than you can understand.

Away with us he's going,
The solemn-eyed:
He'll hear no more the lowing
Of the calves on the warm hillside
Or the kettle on the hob
Sing peace into his breast,
Or see the brown mice bob
Round and round the oatmeal chest.
For he comes, the human child,
To the waters and the wild
With a faery, hand in hand,
From a world more full of weeping than he can understand.

W. B. Yeats

Wednesday's Child

Though bedsore and leech-humoured, I took advice,
coin-hewn, from a hunched, mumping beldam.
She ran yellow nails over his pale flesh, laughed
when I said he was caul-born, gave me waxy ointments,
instructed that I lay his father's coat over him, tie string
on his crib – end to end, sprinkle holy water on the boards,
shoulder-toss salt over the threshold, put a shoe in the rafters,
etch dog Latin on the sill, pillow-stuff my prayers

sleep, sleep, sleep,
your baby will grow
whether you know him or not,
sleep, sleep, sleep,
woe will make your heart slow,
if we cast him back now he'd only rot
weep your eyes dry and
sleep, sleep, sleep

They say his teeth came too soon, I chose the wrong man
to temper him, his name was poor-given, I boasted too much
of his fairness, new clothes are ill-wishes, my milk was tainted,
he supped on sour dreams in my belly.
They say I saw them come and held open the door.
They say,

sleep, sleep, sleep,
your baby will grow
whether you know him or not,
sleep, sleep, sleep,
woe will make your heart slow,
if we cast him back now he'd only rot
weep your eyes dry and
sleep, sleep, sleep

riddle-tongued and cruel, my boy is now a shadow
to the baby in the crib, they say I will feel his fingers
graze my cheek while I sleep

sleep, sleep, sleep

Jo Brandon

Yuki Onna ~ Snow Woman

Clothed in flurries soft as fur,
snow-swathed I stand
head bowed and cradling my baby.

Cold bites with ice-white teeth
as you stop sudden and surprised
on this high mountain road.

Please ... please ...
I offer you the child, but don't explain
I let the strangeness do its work

let you believe there must be logic somewhere,
must be good reason for this ask.
There is.

I suck the pity from your heart,
sweet and sticky as a summer peach.
The baby in your arms is ice now

and you cannot let her go.
Colder than the breath of frost,
more bitter than the deepest North,

your stuttering pulse slows, shudders,
stills to a dead stop.   Done.
And I, Yuki Onna, and my child move on.

Jan Dean

The Siren

'My voice is sweeter than the lute,
My form is passing fair,
My lips are like the scarlet fruit
The coral branches bear.

'My teeth are whiter than the pearls
Men seek beneath the brine,
And when I shake my dripping curls
Far brighter jewels shine;

My russet curls, whose golden tips
Half hide a breast that swells
As pink and pearly as the lips
That laugh on spike-back'd shells;

'My eyes reflect the glimmer cast
When seas lie calm and deep,
Where, under rotting spar and mast,
The silent sailors sleep.

'Oft have I dragged them from the sands, –
They cannot make demur, –
And pull'd the gold rings from their hands:
They neither speak nor stir,

'So stark they lie! Yet one, alone,
Awoke to find me fair, –
(This harp is made of his breast-bone,
Its strings were once his hair!)

'A merry moon we pass'd, and more,
And then upon him came
Some wanton mem'ry of the shore,
He breathed a woman's name;

'Wherefore I made him sleep again,
So sound, he could not stir;
But first I suck'd his heart and brain,
Lest he should dream of her,

'Before he slept he spake strange words;
These were the words he said:
'Your song is blither than the birds',
Your lips are ripe and red,

"Your breast is white, your eyes are blue,
Yet you cannot understand,
Or love your love as the maidens do
That live upon the land.'

'So, since, whene'er the sun is low,
And length'ning shadows fall,
And straying lovers come and go
Along the grey sea-wall,

'Amongst the rocks I crouch me down
To hear what they may say,
And learn this thing I have not known –
To love the land-girls' way!

'But oft I hear them moan and sigh,
And often weep for woe;
The summer nights are going by,
Yet this is all I know!

'So, mine must be the wiser way,
For all my sweetheart said!
I made far merrier than they
The moon that I was wed!

'And he was mine, – my very own!
I clasp'd him firm and fair! ...
(This harp is made of his breast-bone,
Its strings were once his hair!)"

Violet Fane

The Sirens

The sea is lonely, the sea is dreary,
The sea is restless and uneasy;
Thou seekest quiet, thou art weary,
Wandering thou knowest not whither; —
Our little isle is green and breezy,
Come and rest thee! Oh come hither,
Come to this peaceful home of ours,
Where evermore
The low west-wind creeps panting up the shore
To be at rest among the flowers;
Full of rest, the green moss lifts,
As the dark waves of the sea
Draw in and out of rocky rifts,
Calling solemnly to thee
With voices deep and hollow, —
"To the shore
Follow! Oh, follow!
To be at rest forevermore!
Forevermore!"

Look how the gray old Ocean
From the depth of his heart rejoices,
Heaving with a gentle motion,
When he hears our restful voices;
List how he sings in an undertone,
Chiming with our melody;
And all sweet sounds of earth and air
Melt into one low voice alone,
That murmurs over the weary sea,
And seems to sing from everywhere, —
"Here mayst thou harbor peacefully,
Here mayst thou rest from the aching oar;
Turn thy curvèd prow ashore,
And in our green isle rest forevermore!
Forevermore!"
And Echo half wakes in the wooded hill,
And, to her heart so calm and deep,
Murmurs over in her sleep,
Doubtfully pausing and murmuring still,
"Evermore!"
Thus, on Life's weary sea,

Heareth the marinere
Voices sweet, from far and near,
Ever singing low and clear,
Ever singing longingly.
It is not better here to be,
Than to be toiling late and soon?
In the dreary night to see
Nothing but the blood-red moon
Go up and down into the sea;
Or, in the loneliness of day,
To see the still seals only
Solemnly lift their faces gray,
Making it yet more lonely?
Is it not better than to hear
Only the sliding of the wave
Beneath the plank, and feel so near
A cold and lonely grave,
A restless grave, where thou shalt lie
Even in death unquietly?
Look down beneath thy wave-worn bark,
Lean over the side and see
The leaden eye of the sidelong shark
Upturnèd patiently,
Ever waiting there for thee:
Look down and see those shapeless forms,
Which ever keep their dreamless sleep
Far down within the gloomy deep,
And only stir themselves in storms,
Rising like islands from beneath,
And snorting through the angry spray,
As the frail vessel perisheth
In the whirls of their unwieldy play;
Look down! Look down!
Upon the seaweed, slimy and dark,
That waves its arms so lank and brown,
Beckoning for thee!
Look down beneath thy wave-worn bark
Into the cold depth of the sea!
Look down! Look down!
Thus, on Life's lonely sea,
Heareth the marinere

Voices sad, from far and near,
Ever singing full of fear,
Ever singing dreadfully.

Here all is pleasant as a dream;
The wind scarce shaketh down the dew,
The green grass floweth like a stream
Into the ocean's blue;
Listen! Oh, listen!
Here is a gush of many streams,
A song of many birds,
And every wish and longing seems
Lulled to a numbered flow of words, —
Listen! Oh, listen!
Here ever hum the golden bees
Underneath full-blossomed trees,
At once with glowing fruit and flowers crowned; —
So smooth the sand, the yellow sand,
That thy keel will not grate as it touches the land;
All around with a slumberous sound,
The singing waves slide up the strand,
And there, where the smooth, wet pebbles be
The waters gurgle longingly,
As if they fain would seek the shore,
To be at rest from the ceaseless roar,
To be at rest forevermore, —
Forevermore.
Thus, on Life's gloomy sea,
Heareth the marinere
Voices sweet, from far and near,
Ever singing in his ear,
"Here is rest and peace for thee!"

James Russell Lowell

The Erl-King

Who's riding so late through th' endless wild?
The father 'tis with his infant child;
He thinks the boy's well off in his arm,
He grasps him tightly, he keeps him warm.
My son, say why are you hiding your face?
Oh father, the Erlking's coming apace,
The Erlking's here with his train and crown!
My son, the fog moves up and down. –
Be good, my child, come, go with me!
I know nice games, will play them with thee,
And flowers thou'lt find near by where
I live, pretty dress my mother will give."
Dear father, oh father, and do you not hear
What th' Erlking whispers so close to my ear?
Be quiet, do be quiet, my son,
Through leaves the wind is rustling anon.
Do come, my darling, oh come with me!
Good care my daughters will take of thee,
My daughters will dance about thee in a ring,
Will rock thee to sleep and will prettily sing."
Dear father, oh father, and do you not see
The Erlking's daughters so near to me?
My son, my son, no one's in our way,
The willows are looking unusually gray.
I love thee, thy beauty I covet and choose,
Be willing, my darling, or force I shall use!
"Dear father, oh father, he seizes my arm!
The Erlking, father, has done me harm.
The father shudders, he darts through the wild;
With agony fill him the groans of his child.
He reached his farm with fear and dread;
The infant son in his arms was dead.

Johann Wolfgang von Goethe
(trans. Edgar Alfred Bowring)

The Demon Lover

'O where have you been, my dear, dear love,
This long seven years and more?'
'O I'm come to seek my former vows
Ye granted me before.'

'O hold your tongue of your former vows,
For they will breed sad strife;
O hold your tongue of your former vows,
For I am become a wife.'

He turned him right and round about,
And the tear blinded his ee;
'I would never have trodden on Irish ground,
If it had not been for thee.

'I might have had a king's daughtér
Far, far beyond the sea;
I might have had a king's daughtér,
Were it not for love of thee.'

'If ye might have had a king's daughtér,
Yourself ye had to blame;
Ye might have taken the king's daughtér,
For ye kenned that I was nane.

'If I were to leave my husband dear,
And my two babes also,
O what have you to take me to,
If with you I should go?'

'I have seven ships upon the sea,
The eighth brought me to land;
With four and twenty bold mariners,
And music on every hand.'

She has taken up her two little babes,
Kissed them both cheek and chin;
'O fare ye well, my own two babes,
For I'll never see you again.'

She set her foot upon the ship,
No mariners could she behold;
But the sails were of the taffety,
And the masts of the beaten gold.

She had not sailed a league, a league,
A league but barely three,
When dismal grew his countenance,
And drumlie grew his ee.

They had not sailed a league, a league,
A league but barely three,
Until she espied his cloven foot,
And she wept right bitterly

'O hold your tongue of your weeping,' says he,
'Of your weeping now let me be;
I will show you how the lilies grow
On the banks of Italy.'

'O what hills are they, those pleasant hills,
That the sun shines sweetly on?'
'O those are the hills of heaven,' he said,
'Where you will never wone.'

'O whaten a mountain is that,' she said,
'So dreary with frost and snow?'
'O that is the mountain of Hell,' he cried,
'Where you and I must go.'

He struck the top-mast with his hand,
The fore-mast with his knee;
And he brake that gallant ship in twain,
And sank her in the sea.

Anonymous

The Name of the Father

I was diving for oysters when it happened.

Ocean-borne, sea-sheltered,
I would unseal my mouth
to the sweet swell, take it all in.

Then a man came, fretting at flesh
and, dagger-drawn, stripped me to bone,
wolfed me, lip-smacking, raw,

shucked and sucked dry. He was off,
and I sank,
              clinging to sea-bed, tide-
spiralling, in-curling, shell-shocked.

Men do not know the name of Grendel's father.
Women do not need to know.

He made me a monster when he made me a mother:

my brine-baby, my salt-in-the-wound.

Laura Varnam

Like Wolf – and Black Bull or Goblin Hound

Like *wolf* – and black bull or GOBLIN HOUND,
Or come in guise of *spirit*
With WINGS and long *wet waving* hair
And at the FIRE its locks will dry,
Which will be certain SIGN
That one *beneath* the roof must DIE
Before the year's decline
Forget not now what I have *SAID*,
Sit there till we RETURN.
The *hearth* is HOT – watch well the bread
Lest haply it may **burn**.

Charlotte Brontë

Reynardine *(a ballad)*

A basketful of dappled eggs,
    was swaying on my arm,
the sky had darkened to a bog.
    Faint lights picked out our farm.

I'd pinched my cheeks to cloudberries,
    I'd bitten lips to haws,
for disappointing market lads
    who were not worth a pause,

but now in shadow cast by tor,
    I saw him slouching there –
that bold man with his feral smile
    and all that red red hair,

I said 'Kind sir, I ask of you
    please let a poor girl pass,
for I'm alone on this dark mount.'
    The man just blocked my path.

'Dear child,' he said 'I'd never harm
    so much as a pale lamb,'
and I turned pale and fainted, fell
    to arms safe as a den.

Swooning, I felt him muzzle soft,
    then pounce upon my face.
His mouth tasted of meat and moths,
    I writhed in his embrace.

Then pain – his teeth were meat-hook sharp,
    they butchered belly, throat.
He stripped my fingerbones of flesh.
    I screamed. He licked his snout.

And when I managed to come around –
    my innards in his paws –
I begged him weakly: 'What's your name?'
    He laughed. 'I won't be yours –'

'Though you might hunt forevermore,
    through fen, bone-cave or mount.
I live in a dark castle where
    there's everything you want.'

He said his name was Reynardine.
    I'm old with days I've roamed,
but the mountainside is barren,
    and I never get home.

Clare Pollard

A Ballad of the Were-Wolf

The gudewife sits i' the chimney-neuk,
An' looks on the louping flame;
The rain fa's chill, and the win' ca's shrill,
Ere the auld gudeman comes hame.

'Oh, why is your cheek sae wan, gudewife?
An' why do ye glower on me?
Sae dour ye luik i' the chimney-neuk,
Wi' the red licht in your e'e!

'Yet this nicht should ye welcome me,
This ae nicht mair than a',
For I hae scotched yon great grey wolf
That took our bairnies twa.

''Twas a sair, sair strife for my very life,
As I warstled there my lane;
But I'll hae her heart or e'er we part,
Gin ever we meet again.

'An' 'twas ae sharp stroke o' my bonny knife
That gar'd her haud awa';
Fu' fast she went out-owre the bent
Wi'outen her right fore-paw.

'Gae tak' the foot o' the drumlie brute,
And hang it upo' the wa';
An' the next time that we meet, gudewife,
The tane of us shall fa'.'

He's flung his pouch on the gudewife's lap,
    I' the firelicht shinin' fair,
Yet naught they saw o' the grey wolf's paw,
    For a bluidy hand lay there.

O hooly, hooly rose she up,
    Wi' the red licht in her e'e,
Till she stude but a span frae the auld gudeman
    Whiles never a word spak' she.

But she stripped the claiths frae her lang richt arm,
    That were wrappit roun' and roun',
The first was white, an' the last was red;
    And the fresh bluid dreeped adown.

She stretchit him out her lang right arm,
    An' cauld as the deid stude he.
The flames louped bricht i' the gloamin' licht –
    There was nae hand there to see!

Rosamund Marriott Watson

Unwelcome

We were young, we were merry, we were very very wise,
    And the door stood open at our feast,
When there passed us a woman with the West in her eyes,
    And a man with his back to the East.

O, still grew the hearts that were beating so fast,
    The loudest voice was still.
The jest died away on our lips as they passed,
    And the rays of July struck chill.

The cups of red wine turned pale on the board,
    The white bread black as soot.
The hound forgot the hand of her lord,
    She fell down at his foot.

Low let me lie, where the dead dog lies,
    Ere I sit me down again at a feast,
When there passes a woman with the West in her eyes,
    And a man with his back to the East.

Mary Coleridge

The Cat

Within that porch, across the way,
I see two naked eyes this night;
Two eyes that neither shut nor blink,
Searching my face with a green light.

But cats to me are strange, so strange —
I cannot sleep if one is near;
And though I'm sure I see those eyes,
I'm not so sure a body's there!

William Henry Davies

Abduction

The fairy woman walked
into my poem.
She closed no door
She asked no by-your-leave.
Knowing my place
I did not tell her go.
I played the woman-of-no-welcomes trick
and said:

"What's your hurry, here's your hat.
Pull up to the fire,
eat and drink what you get —
but if I were in your house
as you are in my house
I'd go home straight away
but anyway, stay."

She stayed. Got up and pottered
round the house. Dressed the beds
washed the ware. Put the dirty clothes
in the washing-machine.
When my husband came home for his tea
he didn't know what he had wasn't me.

For I am in the fairy field
in lasting darkness
and frozen with the cold there
dressed only in white mist.
And if he wants me back
there is a solution —
get the sock of a plough
smear it with butter
and redden it with fire.

And then let him go to the bed
where lies the succubus
and press her with red iron.
"Push it into her face,
burn and brand her,
and as she fades before your eyes
I'll materialise
and as she fades before your eyes
I'll materialise."

Nuala Ní Dhomhnaill

Lady Isabel and the Elf-Knight

Fair lady Isabel sits in her bower sewing,
Aye as the gowans grow gay
There she heard an elf-knight blawing his horn,
The first morning in May

'If I had yon horn that I hear blawing,
And yon elf-knight to sleep in my bosom.'

This maiden had scarcely these words spoken,
Till in at her window the elf-knight has luppen.

It's a very strange matter, fair maiden,' said he,
'I canna blaw my horn but ye call on me.

'But will ye go to yon greenwood side?
If ye canna gang, I will cause you to ride.'

He leapt on a horse, and she on another,
And they rode on to the greenwood together.

'Light down, light down, lady Isabel,' said he,
'We are come to the place where ye are to die.'

'Hae mercy, hae mercy, kind sir, on me,
Till ance my dear father and mother I see.'

'Seven king's-daughters here hae I slain,
And ye shall be the eight o them.'

'O sit down a while, lay your head on my knee,
That we may hae some rest before that I die.'

She stroakd him sae fast, the nearer he did creep,
Wi a sma charm she lulld him fast asleep.

Wi his ain sword-belt sae fast as she ban him,
Wi his ain dag-durk sae sair as she dang him.

'If seven king's-daughters here ye hae slain.
Lye ye here, a husband to them a'.'

Anonymous (traditional)

Goblin Market (extract)

Laura started from her chair,
Flung her arms up in the air,
Clutched her hair:
"Lizzie, Lizzie, have you tasted
For my sake the fruit forbidden?
Must your light like mine be hidden,
Your young life like mine be wasted,
Undone in mine undoing
And ruined in my ruin,
Thirsty, cankered, goblin-ridden?"—
She clung about her sister,
Kissed and kissed and kissed her:
Tears once again
Refreshed her shrunken eyes,
Dropping like rain
After long sultry drouth;
Shaking with aguish fear, and pain,
She kissed and kissed her with a hungry mouth.

Her lips began to scorch,
That juice was wormwood to her tongue,
She loathed the feast:
Writhing as one possessed she leaped and sung,
Rent all her robe, and wrung
Her hands in lamentable haste,
And beat her breast.
Her locks streamed like the torch
Borne by a racer at full speed,
Or like the mane of horses in their flight,
Or like an eagle when she stems the light
Straight toward the sun,
Or like a caged thing freed,
Or like a flying flag when armies run.

Swift fire spread through her veins, knocked at her heart,
Met the fire smouldering there
And overbore its lesser flame;
She gorged on bitterness without a name:
Ah! fool, to choose such part
Of soul-consuming care!
Sense failed in the mortal strife:
Like the watch-tower of a town
Which an earthquake shatters down,
Like a lightning-stricken mast,
Like a wind-uprooted tree
Spun about,
Like a foam-topped waterspout
Cast down headlong in the sea,
She fell at last;
Pleasure past and anguish past,
Is it death or is it life?

Christina Rossetti

Little Orphan Annie

Little Orphant Annie's come to our house to stay,
An' wash the cups an' saucers up, an' brush the crumbs away,
An' shoo the chickens off the porch, an' dust the hearth, an' sweep,
An' make the fire, an' bake the bread, an' earn her board-an'-keep;
An' all us other children, when the supper-things is done,
We set around the kitchen fire an' has the mostest fun
A-list'nin' to the witch-tales 'at Annie tells about,
An' the Gobble-uns 'at gits you
    Ef you
        Don't
            Watch
                Out!

Wunst they wuz a little boy wouldn't say his prayers, —
An' when he went to bed at night, away up-stairs,
His Mammy heerd him holler, an' his Daddy heerd him bawl,
An' when they turn't the kivvers down, he wuzn't there at all!
An' they seeked him in the rafter-room, an' cubby-hole, an' press,
An' seeked him up the chimbly-flue, an' ever'-wheres, I guess;
But all they ever found wuz thist his pants an' roundabout: —
An' the Gobble-uns 'll git you
    Ef you
        Don't
            Watch
                Out!

An' one time a little girl 'ud allus laugh an' grin,
An' make fun of ever' one, an' all her blood-an'-kin;
An' wunst, when they was "company," an' ole folks wuz there,
She mocked 'em an' shocked 'em, an' said she didn't care!
An' thist as she kicked her heels, an' turn't to run an' hide,
They wuz two great big Black Things a-standin' by her side,
An' they snatched her through the ceilin' 'fore she knowed what she's about!
An' the Gobble-uns 'll git you
    Ef you
        Don't
            Watch
                Out!

An' little Orphant Annie says, when the blaze is blue,
An' the lamp-wick sputters, an' the wind goes woo-oo!
An' you hear the crickets quit, an' the moon is gray,
An' the lightnin'-bugs in dew is all squenched away, —
You better mind yer parunts, an' yer teachurs fond an' dear,
An' churish them 'at loves you, an' dry the orphant's tear,
An' he'p the pore an' needy ones 'at clusters all about,
Er the Gobble-uns 'll git you
Ef you
Don't
Watch
Out!

James Whitcomb Riley

Nine Little Goblins

They all climbed up on a high board-fence —
Nine little Goblins with green-glass eyes —
Nine little Goblins that had no sense,
And couldn't tell coppers from cold mince pies;
And they all climbed up on the fence, and sat —
And I asked them what they were staring at.

And the first one said, as he scratched his head
With a queer little arm that reached out of his ear
And rasped its claws in his hair so red —
"This is what this little arm is fer!"
And he scratched and stared, and the next one said
"How on earth do *you* scratch your head?"

And he laughed like the screech of a rusty hinge —
Laughed and laughed till his face grew black;
And when he choked, with a final twinge
Of his stifling laughter, he thumped his back
With a fist that grew on the end of his tail
Till the breath came back to his lips so pale.

And the third little Goblin leered round at me —
And there were no lids on his eyes at all —
And he clucked one eye, and he says, says he,
"What is the style of your socks this fall?"
And he clapped his heels — and I sighed to see
That he had hands where his feet should be.

Then a bald-faced Goblin, gray and grim,
Bowed his head, and I saw him slip
His eyebrows off, as I looked at him,
And paste them over his upper lip;
And then he moaned in remorseful pain —
"Would — Ah, would I'd me brows again!"

And then the whole of the Goblin band
Rocked on the fence-top to and fro,
And clung, in a long row, hand in hand,
Singing the songs that they used to know —
Singing the songs that their grandsires sung
In the goo-goo days of the Goblin-tongue.

And ever they kept their green-glass eyes
Fixed on me with a stony stare —
Till my own grew glazed with a dread surmise,
And my hat whooped up on my lifted hair,
And I felt the heart in my breast snap-to
As you've heard the lid of a snuff-box do.

And they sang, "You're asleep! There is no board-fence,
And never a Goblin with green-glass eyes! —
'Tis only a vision the mind invents
After a supper of cold mince-pies, —
And you're doomed to dream this way," they said, —
"And you sha'n't wake up till you 're clean plum dead!"

James Whitcomb Riley

The Sphinx

In a dim corner of my room for longer than my fancy thinks
A beautiful and silent Sphinx has watched me through the shifting gloom.

Inviolate and immobile she does not rise she does not stir
For silver moons are naught to her and naught to her the suns that reel.

Red follows grey across the air, the waves of moonlight ebb and flow
But with the Dawn she does not go and in the night-time she is there.

Dawn follows Dawn and Nights grow old and all the while this curious cat
Lies couching on the Chinese mat with eyes of satin rimmed with gold.

Upon the mat she lies and leers and on the tawny throat of her
Flutters the soft and silky fur or ripples to her pointed ears.

Come forth, my lovely seneschal! so somnolent, so statuesque!
Come forth you exquisite grotesque! half woman and half animal!

Come forth my lovely languorous Sphinx! and put your head upon my knee!
And let me stroke your throat and see your body spotted like the Lynx!

And let me touch those curving claws of yellow ivory and grasp
The tail that like a monstrous Asp coils round your heavy velvet paws!

A thousand weary centuries are thine while I have hardly seen
Some twenty summers cast their green for Autumn's gaudy liveries.

But you can read the Hieroglyphs on the great sandstone obelisks,
And you have talked with Basilisks, and you have looked on Hippogriffs.

O tell me, were you standing by when Isis to Osiris knelt?
And did you watch the Egyptian melt her union for Antony

And drink the jewel-drunken wine and bend her head in mimic awe
To see the huge proconsul draw the salted tunny from the brine?

And did you mark the Cyprian kiss white Adon on his catafalque?
And did you follow Amenalk, the God of Heliopolis?

And did you talk with Thoth, and did you hear the moon-horned Io weep?
And know the painted kings who sleep beneath the wedge-shaped Pyramid?

Lift up your large black satin eyes which are like cushions where one sinks!
Fawn at my feet, fantastic Sphinx! and sing me all your memories!

Sing to me of the Jewish maid who wandered with the Holy Child,
And how you led them through the wild, and how they slept beneath your shade.

Sing to me of that odorous green eve when crouching by the marge
You heard from Adrian's gilded barge the laughter of Antinous

And lapped the stream and fed your drouth and watched with hot and hungry stare
The ivory body of that rare young slave with his pomegranate mouth!

Sing to me of the Labyrinth in which the twi-formed bull was stalled!
Sing to me of the night you crawled across the temple's granite plinth

When through the purple corridors the screaming scarlet Ibis flew
In terror, and a horrid dew dripped from the moaning Mandragores,

And the great torpid crocodile within the tank shed slimy tears,
And tare the jewels from his ears and staggered back into the Nile,

And the priests cursed you with shrill psalms as in your claws you seized their snake
And crept away with it to slake your passion by the shuddering palms.

Who were your lovers? who were they who wrestled for you in the dust?
Which was the vessel of your Lust? What Leman had you, every day?

Did giant Lizards come and crouch before you on the reedy banks?
Did Gryphons with great metal flanks leap on you in your trampled couch?

Did monstrous hippopotami come sidling toward you in the mist?
Did gilt-scaled dragons writhe and twist with passion as you passed them by?

And from the brick-built Lycian tomb what horrible Chimera came
With fearful heads and fearful flame to breed new wonders from your womb?

Or had you shameful secret quests and did you harry to your home
Some Nereid coiled in amber foam with curious rock crystal breasts?

Or did you treading through the froth call to the brown Sidonian
For tidings of Leviathan, Leviathan or Behemoth?

Or did you when the sun was set climb up the cactus-covered slope
To meet your swarthy Ethiop whose body was of polished jet?

Or did you while the earthen skiffs dropped down the grey Nilotic flats
At twilight and the flickering bats flew round the temple's triple glyphs

Steal to the border of the bar and swim across the silent lake
And slink into the vault and make the Pyramid your lupanar

Till from each black sarcophagus rose up the painted swathèd dead?
Or did you lure unto your bed the ivory-horned Tragelaphos?

Or did you love the god of flies who plagued the Hebrews and was splashed
With wine unto the waist? or Pasht, who had green beryls for her eyes?

Or that young god, the Tyrian, who was more amorous than the dove
Of Ashtaroth? or did you love the god of the Assyrian

Whose wings, like strange transparent talc, rose high above his hawk-faced head,
Painted with silver and with red and ribbed with rods of Oreichalch?

Or did huge Apis from his car leap down and lay before your feet
Big blossoms of the honey-sweet and honey-coloured nenuphar?

How subtle-secret is your smile! Did you love none then? Nay, I know
Great Ammon was your bedfellow! He lay with you beside the Nile!

The river-horses in the slime trumpeted when they saw him come
Odorous with Syrian galbanum and smeared with spikenard and with thyme.

He came along the river bank like some tall galley argent-sailed,
He strode across the waters, mailed in beauty, and the waters sank.

He strode across the desert sand: he reached the valley where you lay:
He waited till the dawn of day: then touched your black breasts with his hand.

You kissed his mouth with mouths of flame: you made the hornèd god your own:
You stood behind him on his throne: you called him by his secret name.

You whispered monstrous oracles into the caverns of his ears:
With blood of goats and blood of steers you taught him monstrous miracles.

White Ammon was your bedfellow! Your chamber was the steaming Nile!
And with your curved archaic smile you watched his passion come and go.

With Syrian oils his brows were bright: and widespread as a tent at noon
His marble limbs made pale the moon and lent the day a larger light.

His long hair was nine cubits' span and coloured like that yellow gem
Which hidden in their garments' hem the merchants bring from Kurdistan.

His face was as the must that lies upon a vat of new-made wine:
The seas could not insapphirine the perfect azure of his eyes.

His thick soft throat was white as milk and threaded with thin veins of blue:
And curious pearls like frozen dew were broidered on his flowing silk.

On pearl and porphyry pedestalled he was too bright to look upon:
For on his ivory breast there shone the wondrous ocean-emerald,

That mystic moonlit jewel which some diver of the Colchian caves
Had found beneath the blackening waves and carried to the Colchian witch.

Before his gilded galiot ran naked vine-wreathed corybants,
And lines of swaying elephants knelt down to draw his chariot,

And lines of swarthy Nubians bare up his litter as he rode
Down the great granite-paven road between the nodding peacock fans.

The merchants brought him steatite from Sidon in their painted ships:
The meanest cup that touched his lips was fashioned from a chrysolite.

The merchants brought him cedar chests of rich apparel bound with cords;
His train was borne by Memphian lords: young kings were glad to be his guests.

Ten hundred shaven priests did bow to Ammon's altar day and night,
Ten hundred lamps did wave their light through Ammon's carven house – and now

Foul snake and speckled adder with their young ones crawl from stone to stone
For ruined is the house and prone the great rose-marble monolith!

Wild ass or trotting jackal comes and couches in the mouldering gates:
Wild satyrs call unto their mates across the fallen fluted drums.

And on the summit of the pile the blue-faced ape of Horus sits
And gibbers while the fig-tree splits the pillars of the peristyle.

The god is scattered here and there: deep hidden in the windy sand
I saw his giant granite hand still clenched in impotent despair.

And many a wandering caravan of stately negroes silken-shawled,
Crossing the desert, halts appalled before the neck that none can span.

And many a bearded Bedouin draws back his yellow-striped burnous
To gaze upon the Titan thews of him who was thy paladin.

Go, seek his fragments on the moor and wash them in the evening dew,
And from their pieces make anew thy mutilated paramour!

Go, seek them where they lie alone and from their broken pieces make
Thy bruisèd bedfellow! And wake mad passions in the senseless stone!

Charm his dull ear with Syrian hymns! he loved your body! oh, be kind,
Pour spikenard on his hair, and wind soft rolls of linen round his limbs!

Wind round his head the figured coins! stain with red fruits those pallid lips!
Weave purple for his shrunken hips! and purple for his barren loins!

Away to Egypt! Have no fear. Only one God has ever died.
Only one God has let His side be wounded by a soldier's spear.

But these, thy lovers, are not dead. Still by the hundred-cubit gate
Dog-faced Anubis sits in state with lotus-lilies for thy head.

Still from his chair of porphyry gaunt Memnon strains his lidless eyes
Across the empty land, and cries each yellow morning unto thee.

And Nilus with his broken horn lies in his black and oozy bed
And till thy coming will not spread his waters on the withering corn.

Your lovers are not dead, I know. They will rise up and hear your voice
And clash their cymbals and rejoice and run to kiss your mouth! And so,

Set wings upon your argosies! Set horses to your ebon car!
Back to your Nile! Or if you are grown sick of dead divinities

Follow some roving lion's spoor across the copper-coloured plain,
Reach out and hale him by the mane and bid him be your paramour!

Couch by his side upon the grass and set your white teeth in his throat
And when you hear his dying note lash your long flanks of polished brass

And take a tiger for your mate, whose amber sides are flecked with black,
And ride upon his gilded back in triumph through the Theban gate,

And toy with him in amorous jests, and when he turns, and snarls, and gnaws,
O smite him with your jasper claws! and bruise him with your agate breasts!

Why are you tarrying? Get hence! I weary of your sullen ways,
I weary of your steadfast gaze, your somnolent magnificence.

Oscar Wilde

The Hag

The Hag is astride,
This night for to ride;
The Devil and she together:
Through thick and through thin,
Now out and then in,
Though ne'r so foul be the weather.

A thorn or a burr
She takes for a spur:
With a lash of a bramble she rides now,
Through brakes and through briars,
O'er ditches, and mires,
She follows the Spirit that guides now.

No Beast, for his food,
Dares now range the wood;
But hushed in his lair he lies lurking:
While mischiefs, by these,
On land and on seas,
At noon of night are a-working,

The storm will arise
And trouble the skies;
This night, and more for the wonder,
The ghost from the tomb
Affrighted shall come,
Called out by the clap of the thunder.

Robert Herrick

Witchcraft Has Not a Pedigree

Witchcraft has not a pedigree,
'Tis early as our breath,
And mourners meet it going out
The moment of our death.

Emily Dickinson

Witches' Song
(extract from *The Masque of Queens*)

'The Owl is abroad, the Bat, and the Toad,
    And so is the Cat-a-mountain,
The Ant, and the Mole sit both in a hole,
    And Frog peeps out o' the Fountain;
The Dogs, they do bay, and the Timbrels play,
    The Spindle is now a-turning;
The Moon it is red, and the Stars are fled,
    But all the Sky is a-burning.

Ben Jonson

Tam O'Shanter (extract)

Warlocks and witches in a dance;
Nae cotillion brent new frae France,
But hornpipes, jigs, strathspeys, and reels,
Put life and mettle in their heels.
A winnock-bunker in the east,
There sat auld Nick, in shape o' beast;
A towzie tyke, black, grim, and large!
To gie them music was his charge:
He screw'd the pipes and gart them skirl,
Till roof and rafters a' did dirl.
Coffins stood round like open presses,
That shaw'd the dead in their last dresses;
And by some devilish cantraip slight
Each in its cauld hand held a light,
By which heroic Tam was able
To note upon the haly table,
A murderer's banes in gibbet airns;
Twa span-lang, wee, unchristen'd bairns;
A thief, new-cutted frae a rape,
Wi' his last gasp his gab did gape;
Five tomahawks, wi' blude red-rusted;
Five scymitars, wi' murder crusted;
A garter, which a babe had strangled;
A knife, a father's throat had mangled,
Whom his ain son o' life bereft,
The grey hairs yet stack to the heft;
Wi' mair o' horrible and awfu',
Which even to name wad be unlawfu'.

Robert Burns

Macbeth, Act IV, Scene I (extract)

FIRST WITCH

Round about the cauldron go –
In the poisoned entrails throw.
Toad, that under cold stone
Days and nights hast thirty-one,
Sweltered venom sleeping got:
Boil thou first i'th' charmed pot.

ALL

Double, double, toil and trouble,
Fire burn, and cauldron bubble.

SECOND WITCH

Fillet of a fenny snake
In the cauldron boil and bake;
Eye of newt, and toe of frog,
Wool of bat, and tongue of dog,
Adder's fork, and blind-worm's sting,
Lizard's leg, and howlet's wing:
For a charm of powerful trouble,
Like a hell-broth, boil and bubble.

ALL

Double, double, toil and trouble,
Fire burn and cauldron bubble.

THIRD WITCH

Scale of dragon, tooth of wolf,
Witch's mummy, maw and gulf
Of the ravined salt-sea shark;
Root of hemlock, digged i'th' dark;
Liver of blaspheming Jew,
Gall of goat, and slips of yew
Slivered in the moon's eclipse;
Nose of Turk, and Tartar's lips;
Finger of birth-strangled babe
Ditch-delivered by a drab:
Make the gruel thick and slab;
Add thereto a tiger's chawdron,
For th' ingredience of our cauldron.

ALL

Double, double, toil and trouble,
Fire burn and cauldron bubble.

William Shakespeare

War of the Cave

Old Witch, old Witch, come lend me your broom!
Himself is walking the pine-wood's gloom
With Dulcibella, the wench of the farm.
She has a mouse's wit beneath her hair;
We of the craft must have a care
Or he'll take harm.

Old Sloven, Sloven, are you not shamed
Of your sucking Wizard? She's inflamed
To think herself a goddess from his cozening!
She'll teach him flight;
Climb slow before him to a dung-hill's height
And queen it with him for a vassal king.

Ach, you have lost your claws, old Cat!
Time and your sloth have seen to that!
Yet there is virtue in you, *that* I now concede!
By this unwonted courtesy, by this most silly honesty,
I beg a broom of you, though I've no need.

Would you withhold him from me – you a fairy woman?
Can you be jealous, like a puling human?
If he be that fine essence you believe him –
If you, Witch-mother, are not blind and daft –
Now, for the honour of our kind and craft,
I must fly farmwards, to retrieve him.

Your broom, your broom, I say! Give it me quick!
Else I am out, away, on my own stick:
I'll to the zenith with him in straight flight;
Upwards I'll sweep on a fiend-driven wind,
With your sweet changeling pillioned behind,
To dash his carrion from the utmost height!

Anna Wickham

The Weird Gathering (extract)

They've bound the witch with many a thong—
The holy priest is near her;
And ever as she moves along,
A murmur rises hoarse and strong
From those who hate and fear her.
She's standing up for sacrifice,
Beneath the gallows-tree;—
The silent town beneath her lies,
Above her are the Summer skies—
Far off—the quiet sea.
So young—so frail—so very fair—
Why should the victim die?—
Look on her brow!—the red stain there
Burns underneath her tangled hair—
And mark her fiery eye!
A thousand eyes are looking up
In scorn and hate to her;—
A bony hand hath coiled the rope,
And yawns upon the green hill's slope
The witch's sepulchre!
Ha! she hath spurned both priest and book—
Her hand is tossed on high—
Her curse is loud,—she will not brook
The impatient crowd's abiding look—
Hark!—how she shrieks to die!

Up—up—one struggle—all is done!
One groan—the deed is wrought.
Wo—for the wronged and fallen one!—
Her corpse is blackening in the sun—
Her spirit—trace it not!

John Greenleaf Whittier

Witches' Song
(extract from *The Masque of Queens*)

1 WITCH

"I have been all day looking after
A raven feeding upon a quarter:
And, soone as she turn'd her beak to the south,
I snatch'd this morsell out of her mouth."

2 WITCH

"I have beene gathering wolves haires,
The madd dogges foames, and adders eares;
The spurging of a dead man's eyes:
And all since the evening starre did rise."

3 WITCH

"I last night lay all alone
O' the ground, to heare the mandrake grone;
And pluckt him up, though he grew full low:
And, as I had done, the cocke did crow."

4 WITCH

"And I ha' beene chusing out this scull
From charnell houses that were full;
From private grots, and publike pits:
And frighted a sexton out of his wits."

5 WITCH

"Under a cradle I did crepe
By day; and, when the childe was a-sleepe
At night, I suck'd the breath; and rose,
And pluck'd the nodding nurse by the nose.

6 WITCH

"I had a dagger: what did I with that?
Killed an infant to have his fat.
A piper it got at a church-ale.
I bade him again blow wind i' the taile."

7 WITCH

"A murderer yonder was hung in chaines;
The sunne and the wind had shrunke his veins:
I bit off a sinew; I clipp'd his haire;
I brought off his ragges, that danc'd i' the ayre."

8 WITCH

"The scrich-owles egges and the feathers blacke,
The bloud of the frogge, and the bone in his backe
I have been getting; and made of his skin
A purset, to keepe Sir Cranion in."

9 WITCH "And I ha' beene plucking (plants among)
Hemlock, henbane, adders-tongue,
Night-shade, moone-wort, libbards-bane;
And twise by the dogges was like to be tane."

10 WITCH "I from the jaw's of a gardiner's bitch
Did snatch these bones, and then leap'd the ditch:
Yet went I back to the house againe,
Kill'd the blacke cat, and here is the braine."

11 WITCH "I went to the toad, breedes under the wall,
I charmed him out, and he came at my call;
I scratch'd out the eyes of the owle before;
I tore the batts wing: what would you have more?"

DAME "Yes: I have brought, to helpe your vows,
Horned poppie, cypresse boughes,
The fig-tree wild, that grows on tombes,
And juice, that from the larch-tree comes,
The basiliskes bloud, and the vipers skin:–
And now our orgies let's begin."

Ben Jonson

The Broomstick Train, or The Return of the Witches

Look out! Look out, boys! Clear the track!
The witches are here! They've all come back!
They hanged them high, — No use! No use!
What cares a witch for a hangman's noose?
They buried them deep, but they wouldn't lie still,
For cats and witches are hard to kill;
They swore they shouldn't and wouldn't die, —
Books said they did, but they lie! they lie!

— A couple of hundred years, or so,
They had knocked about in the world below,
When an Essex Deacon dropped in to call,
And a homesick feeling seized them all;
For he came from a place they knew full well,
And many a tale he had to tell.
They long to visit the haunts of men,
To see the old dwellings they knew again,
And ride on their broomsticks all around
Their wide domain of unhallowed ground.

In Essex county there's many a roof
Well known to him of the cloven hoof;
The small square windows are full in view
Which the midnight hags went sailing through,
On their well-trained broomsticks mounted high,
Seen like shadows against the sky;
Crossing the track of owls and bats,
Hugging before them their coal-black cats.

Well did they know, those gray old wives,
The sights we see in our daily drives:
Shimmer of lake and shine of sea,
Brown's bare hill with its lonely tree,
(It wasn't then as we see it now,
With one scant scalp-lock to shade its brow);
Dusky nooks in the Essex woods,
Dark, dim, Dante-like solitudes,
Where the tree-toad watches the sinuous snake
Glide through his forests of fern and brake;
Ipswich River; its old stone bridge;

Far off Andover's Indian Ridge,
And many a scene where history tells
Some shadow of bygone terror dwells, —
Of "Norman's Woe" with its tale of dread,
Of the Screeching Woman of Marblehead,
(The fearful story that turns men pale:
Don't bid me tell it, — my speech would fail.)

Who would not, will not, if he can,
Bathe in the breezes of fair Cape Ann, —
Rest in the bowers her bays enfold,
Loved by the sachems and squaws of old?
Home where the white magnolias bloom,
Sweet with the bayberry's chaste perfume,
Hugged by the woods and kissed by the sea!
Where is the Eden like to thee?

For that "couple of hundred years, or so,"
There had been no peace in the world below;
The witches still grumbling, "It isn't fair;
Come, give us a taste of the upper air!
We've had enough of your sulphur springs,
And the evil odor that round them clings;
We long for a drink that is cool and nice, —
Great buckets of water with Wenham ice;
We've served you well up-stairs, you know;
You're a good old fellow — come, let us go!"

I don't feel sure of his being good,
But he happened to be in a pleasant mood, —
As fiends with their skins full sometimes are, —
(He'd been drinking with "roughs" at a Boston bar).
So what does he do but up and shout
To a graybeard turnkey, "Let 'em out!"

To mind his orders was all he knew;
The gates swung open, and out they flew.
"Where are our broomsticks?" the beldams cried.
"Here are your broomsticks," an imp replied.
"They've been in — the place you know — so long
They smell of brimstone uncommon strong;

But they've gained by being left alone, —
Just look, and you'll see how tall they've grown."
"And where is my cat?" a vixen squalled.
"Yes, where are our cats?" the witches bawled,
And began to call them all by name:
As fast as they called the cats, they came:
There was bob-tailed Tommy and long-tailed Tim,
And wall-eyed Jacky and green-eyed Jim,
And splay-foot Benny and slim-legged Beau,
And Skinny and Squally, and Jerry and Joe,
And many another that came at call, —
It would take too long to count them all.
All black, — one could hardly tell which was which,
But every cat knew his own old witch;
And she knew hers as hers knew her, —
Ah, didn't they curl their tails and purr!

No sooner the withered hags were free
Than out they swarmed for a midnight spree;
I couldn't tell all they did in rhymes,
But the Essex people had dreadful times.
The Swampscott fishermen still relate
How a strange sea-monster stole their bait;
How their nets were tangled in loops and knots,
And they found dead crabs in their lobster-pots.
Poor Danvers grieved for her blasted crops, —
And Wilmington mourned over mildewed hops.
A blight played havoc with Beverly beans, —
It was all the work of those hateful queans!
A dreadful panic began at "Pride's,"
Where the witches stopped in their midnight rides,
And there rose strange rumors and vague alarms
'Mid the peaceful dwellers at Beverly Farms.

Now when the Boss of the Beldams found
That without his leave they were ramping round,
He called, — they could hear him twenty miles,
From Chelsea beach to the Misery Isles;
The deafest old granny knew his tone
Without the trick of the telephone.
"Come here, you witches! Come here!" says he, —

“At your games of old, without asking me!
I’ll give you a little job to do
That will keep you stirring, you godless crew!”

They came, of course, at their master’s call,
The witches, the broomsticks, the cats, and all;
He led the hags to a railway train
The horses were trying to drag in vain.
“Now, then,” says he, “you’ve had your fun,
And here are the cars you’ve got to run.
The driver may just unhitch his team,
We don’t want horses, we don’t want steam;
You may keep your old black cats to hug,
But the loaded train you’ve got to lug.”

Since then on many a car you’ll see
A broomstick plain as plain can be;
On every stick there’s a witch astride, —
The string you see to her leg is tied.
She will do a mischief if she can,
But the string is held by a careful man,
And whenever the evil-minded witch
Would cut some caper, he gives a twitch.
As for the hag, you can’t see her,
But hark! you can hear her black cat’s purr,
And now and then, as a car goes by,
You may catch a gleam from her wicked eye.

Often you’ve looked on a rushing train,
But just what moved it was not so plain.
It couldn’t be those wires above,
For they could neither pull nor shove;
Where was the motor that made it go
You couldn’t guess, ***but now you know.***

Remember my rhymes when you ride again
On the rattling rail by the broomstick train!

Oliver Wendell Holmes

Young Man Naughty's Adventure

Murk was the night: nor star, nor moon,
 Shone in the cloud-wrapped sky,
To break the dull, tenebrous gloom
 Of the arched vault on high,

When Naughty, with his dog and gun,
 Walked lonely o'er the moor;
True, the shooting-season had not begun, –
 But poachers commence before!

The howling winds blew fierce around,
 The rain drove in his face;
And, as Naughty heard the hollow sound,
 He quickened his creeping pace.

For as each hoarse sepulchral blast
 Drew slow and solemn near,
It seemed like spirits sailing past
 To his affrighted ear.

For he was on a dreadful errand bent
 To the ancient witch of the moor;
A delegate by his comrades sent
 To consult the beldam hoar.

Now yelled the wind with more terrible din,
 Now rattled the rain full fast;
And, noiselessly gliding, forms were seen,
 As around his eyes he cast;

When a rustling sound in the heather he heard:
 Starting, he turned about;
Was it a spirit? Was it a bird?
 No! a hare sprang trembling out.

The shot went 'Whizz!' and the gun went 'Bang!'
 A flash illumined the air;
Far and wide the moor with the echo rang
 As down dropped the luckless hare.

He ran to the spot, and, lo! there lay
 A woman on the hard heath-bed,
Whose soul had left its breathless clay,
 For the witch of the moor was dead!

Charlotte Brontë

Medea Casts a Spell to Make Aeson Young Again
(extract from *Metamorphoses*)

Medea with her hair not trussed so much as in a lace,
But flaring on her shoulders twain, and barefoot, with her gown
Ungirded, got her out of doors and wandered up and down
Alone the dead time of the night: both man, and beast, and bird
Were fast asleep: the serpents sly in trailing forward stirred
So softly that you would have thought they still asleep had been.
The moisting air was whist: no leaf ye could have moving seen.
The stars alonely fair and bright did in the welkin shine.
To which she, lifting up her hands, did thrice herself incline,
And thrice with water of the brook her hair besprinkled she:
And gasping thrice she oped her mouth: and bowing down her knee
Upon the bare hard ground, she said: 'Oh trusty time of night,
Most faithful unto privities, oh golden stars whose light
Doth jointly with the moon succeed the beams that blaze by day,
And thou, three-headed Hecate, who knowest best the way
To compass this our great attempt, and art our chiefest stay:
Ye charms and witchcrafts, and thou earth which both with herb and weed
Of mighty working furnishest the wizards at their need:
Ye airs and winds: ye elves of hills, of brooks, of woods alone,
Of standing lakes, and of the night, approach ye everychone.
Through help of whom (the crooked banks much wondering at the thing)
I have compellèd streams to run clean backward to their spring.
By charms I make the calm seas rough, and make the rough seas plain,
And cover all the sky with clouds, and chase them hence again.
By charms I raise and lay the winds, and burst the viper's jaw,
And from the bowels of the earth both stones and trees do draw.
Whole woods and forests I remove: I make the mountains shake,
And even the earth itself to groan and fearfully to quake.
I call up dead men from their graves: and thee, oh lightsome moon,
I darken oft, though beaten brass abate thy peril soon:
Our sorcery dims the morning fair, and darks the sun at noon.

Ovid (trans. Arthur Golding)

Circe (extract)

Too cruel, am I? And the silly beasts,
Crowding around me when I pass their way,
Glower on me and, although they love me still,
(With their poor sorts of love such as they could)
Call wrath and vengeance to their humid eyes
To scare me into mercy, or creep near
With piteous fawnings, supplicating bleats.
Too cruel? Did I choose them what they are?
Or change them from themselves by poisonous charms?
But any draught, pure water, natural wine,
Out of my cup, revealed them to themselves
And to each other. Change? there was no change;
Only disguise gone from them unawares:
And had there been one true right man of them
He would have drunk the draught as I had drunk,
And stood unharmed and looked me in the eyes,
Abashing me before him. But these things –
Why, which of them has even shown the kind
Of some one nobler beast? Pah! yapping wolves,
And pitiless stealthy wild-cats, curs, and apes,
And gorging swine, and slinking venomous snakes –
All false and ravenous and sensual brutes
That shame the Earth that bore them, these they are.

Augusta Webster

Sonnets from a Lock Box (extract)

XXV

Into the void behold my shuddering flight,
Plunging straight forward through unhuman space,
My wild hair backward blown and my white face
Set like a wedge of ice. My chattering teeth
Cut like sharp knives my swiftly freezing breath.
Perched upon straightness I seek a wilder zone.
My Flying Self – on this black steed alone –
Drives out to God or else to utter death.
Beware straight lines which do subdue man's pride!
'Tis on a broomstick that great witches ride.
Wild, dangerous and holy are the runes
Which shift the whirling atoms with their tunes.
Oh like a witch accursed shall she be burned
Who having flown on straightness has returned.

Anna Hempstead Branch

For the Wine of Circe by Edward Burne Jones

Dusk-haired and gold-robed o'er the golden wine
    She stoops, wherein, distilled of death and shame,
    Sink the black drops; while, lit with fragrant flame,
Round her spread board the golden sunflowers shine.
Doth Helios here with Hecatè combine
    (O Circe, thou their votaress?) to proclaim
    For these thy guests all rapture in Love's name,
Till pitiless Night give Day the countersign?
Lords of their hour, they come. And by her knee
    Those cowering beasts, their equals heretofore,
Wait; who with them in new equality
    To-night shall echo back the sea's dull roar
    With a vain wail from passion's tide-strown shore
Where the disheveled seaweed hates the sea.

Dante Gabriel Rossetti

Her Kind

I have gone out, a possessed witch,
haunting the black air, braver at night;
dreaming evil, I have done my hitch
over the plain houses, light by light:
lonely thing, twelve-fingered, out of mind.
A woman like that is not a woman, quite.
I have been her kind.

I have found the warm caves in the woods,
filled them with skillets, carvings, shelves,
closets, silks, innumerable goods;
fixed the suppers for the worms and the elves:
whining, rearranging the disaligned.
A woman like that is misunderstood.
I have been her kind.

I have ridden in your cart, driver,
waved my nude arms at villages going by,
learning the last bright routes, survivor
where your flames still bite my thigh
and my ribs crack where your wheels wind.
A woman like that is not ashamed to die.
I have been her kind.

Anne Sexton

The Heavenly Bitch (extract)

Master, O master, turn to me, speak!
Why do you wander, and what do you seek
Long on the edge of this foetid lake?
Come with me, come for your leman's sake.
We drowned a priest in that horrible hole,
And weighted his corpse with a live man's soul.
The air is thick with his odious stink:
O walk no more by the deathly brink.

Master, O master, why do you stare?
What do you see on the lake out there?
It's only a clot of floating weed.
Why do you wait? O will you not heed!
In the mud of the lake, a saint lies dead
With a live man's soul for a stone at his head.

It is no weed looks up at the sky
As if the mere were a beast with one eye.
This is my winnings, this my reward,
That my soul is tied to a stretching cord,
To the rotting flesh of a silly priest:
It has mounted to air like a bubble in yeast;
It is mocked at noon by the high hot light,
And stars invade its void by night.
Girl, my girl, I would have it again.
My flesh dissolves to ash with pain.

Master, O master, am I not your witch?
See! I am transformed to an old black bitch;
So I run swift through the menacing night
To your cave, to your shelter, to your delight.
And I am a valiant swimmer, my lord:
I will fetch the stone for love's reward.

I'll swim to the saint, and swim to the land,
And lay the stone in my master's hand.
For, if my lord would climb to their Heaven,
Importunate doors of the sky shall be riven;
A bitch shall lurk at god's high gate
And yap and yap at his solemn state
Till she wreck God's peace with her tireless din
And Saints shall open and let her man in.

Anna Wickham

The Burning

It was the hard winter she came,
frozen larks plummeting through the gloam like falling stars,
each pail in the yard a slattern's looking glass.

Each dusk, the house cobwebbed by creeping frost,
my husband slipped like a knife from an oyster,
my sons nestled like dormice in their cots,
I stood at my black window and oh
the cold it pressed upon me like a lover,
held its hands to my throat, my knees.

She came first through the trees:
a small glint amongst the poplars,
hoarfrost dripping from the velvet nubs of their antlers,
leaping fast to a shuddering pillar of flame,
her pelvis a cradle of jeweled tinder,
her ribs white kindling. A holy thing—
such furious unblossoming—and something profane.

I pressed my eye to the glass, the crackling dark,
saw her heart catch light,
blackbirds flap frantic from the forks of trees—
—woke shivering, sweat between my breasts,
my tongue in my teeth.

Every night then she came
in the stolen hours between caring and dream,
the children vanished, the drudging chaos of day
put to sleep.
I have no words to tell of the shapes she scorched,
the frozen lock, the copper key,
but that heat licked me raw as a wild love,
cracked the ice on my ribs and tossed in a flare.

All my life I have been a good woman,
compliant, neat, my children's snow boots polished,
each snowflake of ash swept clean from my step.

I've worn obedience like a uniform,
the hoof of the iron cooling in my grate.
Yet I riled in the witching hour, tongue glittering.
My darling, I whispered to my own dry bones,
for what do you burn?

Three moons she has been absent,
though I wait at my window, the chill persisting, presaging snow,
and my longing rises hopeless as the carp in the pool.
I don't know where she is living
or if she lives at all—
with women nursing in fevered sheets
or scrubbing floors until their knuckles ignite?

But by dark, when my sons sail the black cut
of sleep, and frost lays its terrible lace
upon the grass, when I am alone with my fretting,
with my dreams like black pearls in the clam of my mouth,
I press my fists to that tenderest wound—my soul—
and Christ how I burn.

Liz Berry

The Witch

I have walked a great while over the snow,
And I am not tall nor strong.
My clothes are wet, and my teeth are set,
And the way was hard and long.
I have wandered over the fruitful earth,
But I never came here before.
Oh, lift me over the threshold, and let me in at the door!

The cutting wind is a cruel foe.
I dare not stand in the blast.
My hands are stone, and my voice a groan,
And the worst of death is past.
I am but a little maiden still,
My little white feet are sore.
Oh, lift me over the threshold, and let me in at the door!

Her voice was the voice that women have,
Who plead for their heart's desire.
She came – she came – and the quivering flame
Sunk and died in the fire.
It never was lit again on my hearth
Since I hurried across the floor,
To lift her over the threshold, and let her in at the door.

Mary Coleridge

The Witch Bride

A fair witch crept to a young man's side,
And he kiss'd her and took her for his bride.

But a Shape came in at the dead of night,
And fill'd the room with snowy light.

And he saw how in his arms there lay
A thing more frightful than mouth may say.

And he rose in haste, and follow'd the Shape
Till morning crown'd an eastern cape.

And he girded himself, and follow'd still,
When sunset sainted the western hill.

But, mocking and thwarting, clung to his side,
Weary day! – the foul Witch-Bride.

William Allingham

Hallowe'en: Or, A Tale of Terror

The night it was gloomy, the Croghan it lour'd,
As MacUilin traversed the Banks of the Mourne;
In torrents the rain, rude and pitiless, pour'd
As by Hallowe'en Fancy, his footsteps were borne.

For his heart was the prey of sad joyless despair,
Since Celia, his passion insulting reprov'd,
And he swore he'd lose all in the magical sphere,
To force to his bosom the fair that he lov'd.

Tho' the tempest was howling, and starless the sky,
He dreaded no dangers, he fear'd not the storm;
But he silently pray'd that his gloom piercing eye
Might soon have a glimpse of her fanciful form.

Near the mouldering walls of an Abbey he strayed,
There, thrice he invok'd the foul demon of Air;
Then a flowerless sod o'er his shoulder he laid,
And seal'd with his blood the unsanctified prayer.

His rites scarce had ceased, when lo, in the gloom
On the ivy clad walls a blue flame he descried;
He trembled as down by the ash coloured broom,
A pale ghastly phantom towards him did glide.

'Twas not the sweet phantom of Celia was nigh;
But a Gnomon of Hell met his horror-struck view;
"I come," cried the Fiend, with a heart-rending cry,
"Invoked by your spells to be wedded to you.

Long and sad was I chain'd in the venomous dell,
Till, thrice you invoked the Spirit of Air;
And your blood on the parchment confirmed the spell,
Now with me you'll fly to the Gulph of Despair."

Then the merciless Fangs close encircled his arms,
And she told him a tale which no mortal could tell;
How his Hallowe'en freaks and his magical charms,
Had doom'd him fore'er to the cavern of Hell.

Then ghastly she smil'd, "never more shall we sunder,
Ne'er again to the world shall your footsteps return."
Then she tore out his heart with a yell loud as thunder,
And headlong both plunged into dark-rolling Mourne.

Revi

Body's Beauty
(extract from *The House of Life*)

LXXVIII

Of Adam's first wife, Lilith, it is told
    (The witch he loved before the gift of Eve,)
    That, ere the snake's, her sweet tongue could deceive,
And her enchanted hair was the first gold.
And still she sits, young while the earth is old,
    And, subtly of herself contemplative,
    Draws men to watch the bright web she can weave,
Till heart and body and life are in its hold.

The rose and poppy are her flowers; for where
    Is he not found, O Lilith, whom shed scent
And soft-shed kisses and soft sleep shall snare?
    Lo! as that youth's eyes burned at thine, so went
    Thy spell through him, and left his straight neck bent
And round his heart one strangling golden hair.

Dante Gabriel Rossetti

Carrefour

O You,
Who came upon me once
Stretched under apple-trees just after bathing,
Why did you not strangle me before speaking
Rather than fill me with the wild white honey of your words
And then leave me to the mercy
Of the forest bees.

Amy Lowell

Angela Damnifera

Could I have known, that day I saw you first,
    How much my fate lay coiled within your eyes!
    How Nemesis spoke in your soft replies!
Could I have known – and so have shunned the worst?
Could I have known how for my bitter thirst
    Your coming brought but saltest tears and sighs,
    How going life seemed fled with you likewise.
Could I have known – oh angel love-accurs'd!

And now how name you, slayer of my peace?
    Life-giving basilisk? source of gladdest woe?
    Emblem of Fortune wrecked upon one throw?
O'er blessed and damned flame-hallowed Beatrice?
And cause of martyrdom without surcease?
    Alas! Alas! by me entreated so!

Ford Madox Brown

The Amber Witch

I went across the twilight moor,
Through pine woods purply glimmering,
I heard, not half a league before,
The glad sea sing.

The glad, glad sea sang low to me,
And how I answered, stooping blind
Through brake and bough, till every tree
Lay dark behind.

From out the moon-soaked sleepy sands,
With vacant laughter, like a fool,
The sea had scooped with his two hands
A green, green pool.

All naked on a pale green stone,
Where circling water-snakes burned rich,
Sat waiting eager-eyed and lone,
The amber witch.

She drew my hand upon her knee,
About my body everywhere
The bright snakes burned, and over me
Drooped her wild hair.

Her body swayed into a tune,
Her lips were writhen as with pain,
Her eyes swam dim while she did croon
A dim, dim strain.

I stooped into the wood black-pined,
I startled at the moon-bright moor,
I heard, not half a league behind,
The mad sea roar.

The mad sea clamored hoarse on me,
And nought I answered, lest the moon
Should let her amber hair float free,
And stoop, and croon.

William Vaughn Moody

La Belle Dame sans Merci

O what can ail thee, Knight at arms,
Alone and palely loitering?
The sedge has withered from the Lake
And no birds sing!

O what can ail thee, Knight at arms,
So haggard, and so woebegone?
The squirrel's granary is full
And the harvest's done.

I see a lily on thy brow
With anguish moist and fever dew,
And on thy cheeks a fading rose
Fast withereth too.

"I met a lady in the Meads,
Full beautiful, a faery's child,
Her hair was long, her foot was light
And her eyes were wild.

"I made a Garland for her head,
And bracelets too, and fragrant Zone;
She looked at me as she did love
And made sweet moan.

"I set her on my pacing steed
And nothing else saw all day long,
For sidelong would she bend and sing
A faery's song.

"She found me roots of relish sweet,
And honey wild, and manna dew,
And sure in language strange she said
'I love thee true'.

"She took me to her elfin grot,
And there she wept and sighed full sore,
And there I shut her wild wild eyes
With kisses four.

"And there she lullèd me asleep,
    And there I dreamed, Ah Woe betide!
The latest dream I ever dreamt
    On the cold hill side.

"I saw pale Kings and Princes too,
    Pale warriors, death-pale were they all;
They cried, 'La belle dame sans merci
    Hath thee in thrall!'

"I saw their starved lips in the gloam
    With horrid warning gapèd wide,
And I awoke, and found me here
    On the cold hill's side.

"And this is why I sojourn here,
    Alone and palely loitering;
Though the sedge is withered from the Lake
    And no birds sing."

John Keats

Her Strong Enchantments Failing

Her strong enchantments failing,
  Her towers of fear in wreck,
Her limbecks dried of poisons
  And the knife at her neck,

The Queen of air and darkness
  Begins to shrill and cry,
'O young man, O my slayer,
  To-morrow you shall die.'

O Queen of air and darkness,
  I think 'tis truth you say,
And I shall die to-morrow;
  But you will die to-day.

A. E. Housman

Song for the Clatter-Bones

God rest that wicked woman,
Queen Jezebel, the bitch
Who peeled the clothes from her shoulder-bones
Down to her spent teats
As she stretched out of the window
Among the geraniums, where
She chaffed and laughed like one half daft
Titivating her painted hair –

King Jehu he drove to her,
She tipped him a fancy beck;
But he from his knacky side-car spoke,
'Who'll break that dewlapped neck?'
And so she was thrown from the window;
Like Lucifer she fell
Beneath the feet of the horses and they beat
The light out of Jezebel.

That corpse wasn't planted in clover;
Ah, nothing of her was found
Save those grey bones that Hare-foot Mike
Gave me for their lovely sound;
And as once her dancing body
Made star-lit princes sweat,
So I'll just clack: though her ghost lacks a back
There's music in the old bones yet.

F. R. Higgins

False, but Beautiful

Dark as a demon's dream is one I love—
In soul—but oh, how beautiful in form!
She glows like Venus throned in joy above,
Or on the crimson couch of Evening warm
Reposing her sweet limbs, her heaving breast
Unveiled to him who lights the golden west!
Ah, me, to be by that soft hand carest,
To feel the twining of that snowy arm,
To drink that sigh with richest love opprest,
To bathe within that sunny sea of smiles,
To wander in that wilderness of wiles
And blissful blandishments—it is to thrill
With subtle poison, and to feel the will
Grow weak in that which all the veins doth fill.
Fair sorceress! I know she spreads a net
The strong, the just, the brave to snare; and yet
My soul cannot, for its own sake, forget
The fascinating glance which flings its chain
Around my quivering heart and throbbing brain,
And binds me to my painful destiny,
As bird, that soars no more on high,
Hangs trembling on the serpent's doomful eye.

John Rollin Ridge

Fletcher McGee

She took my strength by minutes,
She took my life by hours,
She drained me like a fevered moon
That saps the spinning world.
The days went by like shadows,
The minutes wheeled like stars.
She took the pity from my heart,
And made it into smiles.
She was a hunk of sculptor's clay,
My secret thoughts were fingers
They flew behind her pensive brow
And lined it deep with pain.
They set the lips, and sagged the cheeks,
And drooped the eyes with sorrow.
My soul had entered in the clay,
Fighting like seven devils.
It was not mine, it was not hers;
She held it, but its struggles
Modeled a face she hated,
And a face I feared to see.
I beat the windows, shook the bolts.
I hid me in a corner—
And then she died and haunted me,
And hunted me for life.

Edgar Lee Masters

The Card-Dealer

Could you not drink her gaze like wine?
    Yet, though its splendour swoon
Into the silence languidly
    As a tune into a tune,
Those eyes unravel the coiled night
    And know the stars at noon.

The gold that's heaped beside her hand,
    In truth rich prize it were;
And rich the dreams that wreathe her brows
    With magic stillness there;
And he were rich who should unwind
    That woven golden hair.

Around her, where she sits, the dance
    Now breathes its eager heat;
And not more lightly or more true
    Fall there the dancers' feet
Than fall her cards on the bright board
    As 'twere an heart that beat.

Her fingers let them softly through,
    Smooth-polished silent things;
And each one as it falls reflects
    In swift light-shadowings,
Blood-red and purple, green and blue,
    The great eyes of her rings.

Whom plays she with? With thee, who lov'st
    Those gems upon her hand;
With me, who search her secret brows;
    With all men, bless'd or bann'd.
We play together, she and we,
    Within a vain strange land:

A land without any order, –
    Day even as night, (one saith,) –
Where who lieth down ariseth not
    Nor the sleeper awakeneth;
A land of darkness as darkness itself
    And of the shadow of death.

What be her cards, you ask? Even these–
    The heart, that doth but crave
More, having fed; the diamond,
    Skilled to make base seem brave;
The club, for smiting in the dark;
    The spade, to dig a grave.

And do you ask what game she plays?
    With me 'tis lost or won;
With thee it is playing still; with him
    It is not well begun;
But 'tis a game she plays with all
    Beneath the sway o' the sun.

Thou seest the card that falls, – she knows
    The card that followeth:
Her game in thy tongue is called Life,
    As ebbs thy daily breath:
When she shall speak, thou'lt learn her tongue
    And know she calls it Death.

Dante Gabriel Rossetti

Babylon the Great

Foul is she and ill-favoured, set askew:
Gaze not upon her till thou dream her fair,
Lest she should mesh thee in her wanton hair,
Adept in arts grown old yet ever new.
Her heart lusts not for love, but thro' and thro'
For blood, as spotted panther lusts in lair;
No wine is in her cup, but filth is there
Unutterable, with plagues hid out of view.
Gaze not upon her; for her dancing whirl
Turns giddy the fixed gazer presently:
Gaze not upon her, lest thou be as she
When at the far end of her long desire
Her scarlet vest and gold and gem and pearl
And she amid her pomp are set on fire.

Christina Rossetti

Laus Veneris (extract)

Their blood runs round the roots of time like rain:
She casts them forth and gathers them again;
    With nerve and bone she weaves and multiplies
Exceeding pleasure out of extreme pain.

Her little chambers drip with flower-like red,
Her girdles, and the chaplets of her head.
    Her armlets and her anklets; with her feet
She tramples all that winepress of the dead.

Her gateways smoke with fume of flowers and fires,
With loves burnt out and unassuaged desires;
    Between her lips the steam of them is sweet,
The languor in her ears of many lyres.

Her beds are full of perfume and sad sound,
Her doors are made with music, and barred round
    With sighing and with laughter and with tears,
With tears whereby strong souls of men are bound.

There is the knight Adonis that was slain;
With flesh and blood she chains him for a chain;
    The body and the spirit in her ears
Cry, for her lips divide him vein by vein.

Yea, all she slayeth; yea, every man save me;
Me, love, thy lover that must cleave to thee
    Till the ending of the days and ways of earth,
The shaking of the sources of the sea.

Me, most forsaken of all souls that fell;
Me, satiated with things insatiable;
    Me, for whose sake the extreme hell makes mirth,
Yea, laughter kindles at the heart of hell.

Algernon Charles Swinburne

The Vampire

A lily in a twilight place?
A moonflow'r in the lonely night?—
Strange beauty of a woman's face
Of wildflow'r-white!

The rain that hangs a star's green ray
Slim on a leaf-point's restlessness,
Is not so glimmering green and gray
As was her dress.

I drew her dark hair from her eyes,
And in their deeps beheld a while
Such shadowy moonlight as the skies
Of Hell may smile.

She held her mouth up redly wan,
And burning cold,—I bent and kissed
Such rosy snow as some wild dawn
Makes of a mist.

God shall not take from me that hour,
When round my neck her white arms clung!
When 'neath my lips, like some fierce flower,
Her white throat swung!

Or words she murmured while she leaned!
Witch-words, she holds me softly by,—
The spell that binds me to a fiend
Until I die.

Madison Cawein

The Vampire Bride

"I am come—I am come! once again from the tomb,
In return for the ring which you gave;
That I am thine, and that thou art mine,
This nuptial pledge receive."

He lay like a corse 'neath the Demon's force,
And she wrapp'd him in a shround;
And she fixed her teeth his heart beneath,
And she drank of the warm life-blood!

And ever and anon murmur'd the lips of stone,
"Soft and warm is this couch of thine,
Thou'lt to-morrow be laid on a colder bed—
Albert! that bed will be mine!"

Henry Thomas Liddell

The Vampire

I

I found a corpse, with glittering hair,
of a woman whose face, tho' dead,
The white death in it had left still fair
Too fair for an earthly bed!
So I loosened each fold of her bright curls roll'd
From forehead to foot in a rush of red gold,
And kissed her lips till her lips were red,
And warm and light on her eyelids white
I breath'd, and pressed unto mine her breast,
Till the blue eyes oped and the breast grew warm,
And this woman, behold! arose up bold,
And lifelike lifting a wilful arm,
With steady feet from the winding sheet
Stepp'd forth to a mutter'd charm.

II

And now beside me, whatever betide me,
This woman is, night and day.
For she cleaves to me so, that, wherever I go
She is with me the whole of the way.
And her eyes are so bright in the dead of the night,
That they keep me awake with dread;
While my life blood pales in my veins and fails,
Because her red lips are so red
That I fear 'tis my heart she must eat for her food;
And it makes my whole flesh creep
To think she is drinking and draining my blood,
Unawares, if I chance to sleep.

III

It were better for me, ere I came nigh her, –
    This corpse, – ere I looked upon her, –
Had they burn'd my body with penal fire
    With a sorcerer's dishonour.
For when the devil has made his lair
    In the living eyes of a dear dead woman,
(To bind a man's strength by her golden hair,
    And break his heart, if his heart be human),
Is there any penance, or any prayer,
    That may save the sinner whose soul he tries
To catch in the curse of the constant stare
    Of those heartbreaking bewildering eyes, –
Comfortless, cavernous glowworms that glare
    From the gaping grave where a dead hope lies?
It is more than the soul of a man may bear.
    For the misery worst of all miseries
Is Desire eternally feeding Despair
    On the flesh, or the blood, that forever supplies
Life more than enough to keep fresh in repair
    The death ever dying, which yet never dies.

Owen Meredith, Lord Lytton

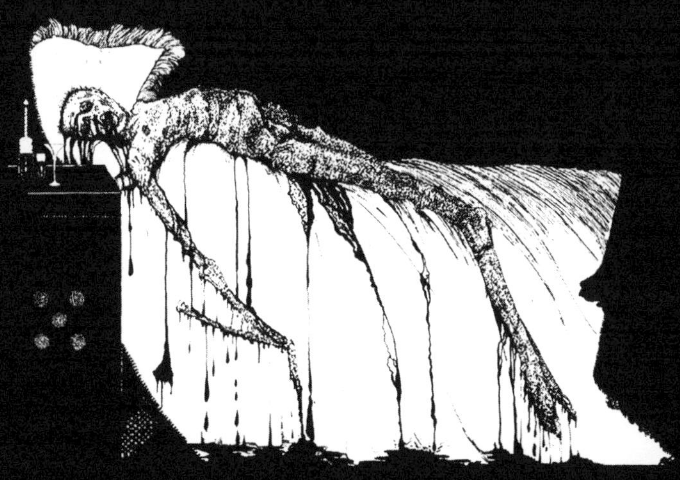

The Giaour (excerpt)

… unquenched, unquenchable,
Around, within, thy heart shall dwell;
Nor ear can hear nor tongue can tell
The tortures of that inward hell!
But first, on earth as vampire sent,
Thy corse shall from its tomb be rent:
Then ghastly haunt thy native place,
And suck the blood of all thy race;
There from thy daughter, sister, wife,
At midnight drain the stream of life;
Yet loathe the banquet which perforce
Must feed thy livid living corse:
Thy victims ere they yet expire
Shall know the demon for their sire,
As cursing thee, thou cursing them,
Thy flowers are withered on the stem.
But one that for thy crime must fall,
The youngest, most beloved of all,
Shall bless thee with a father's name –
That word shall wrap thy heart in flame!
Yet must thou end thy task, and mark
Her cheek's last tinge, her eye's last spark,
And the last glassy glance must view
Which freezes o'er its lifeless blue;
Then with unhallowed hand shalt tear
The tresses of her yellow hair,
Of which in life a lock when shorn
Affection's fondest pledge was worn,
But now is borne away by thee,
Memorial of thine agony!

George Gordon, Lord Byron

The Vampire

My dear young maiden clingeth
Unbending fast and firm
To all the long-held teaching
Of a mother ever true;
As in vampires unmortal
Folk on the Theyse's portal
Heyduck-like do believe.
But my Christine thou dost dally,
And wilt my loving parry
Till I myself avenging
To a vampire's health a-drinking
Him toast in pale tockay.

And as softly thou art sleeping
To thee shall I come creeping
And thy life's blood drain away.
And so shalt thou be trembling
For thus shall I be kissing
And death's threshold thou'lt be crossing
With fear, in my cold arms.
And last shall I thee question
Compared to such instruction
What are a mother's charms?

Heinrich August Ossenfelder

The Vampyre (extract)

"Why looks my lord so deadly pale?
Why fades the crimson from his cheek?
What can my dearest husband ail?
Thy heartfelt cares, O Herman, speak!

"Restless, tho' sleeping, still you groan,
And with convulsive horror start;
O Herman! to thy wife make known
That grief which preys upon thy heart."

"O Gertrude, 'tis a horrid cause,
O Gertrude, 'tis unusual care,
That, vulture-like, my vitals gnaws,
And galls my bosom with despair.

"Young Sigismund, my once dear friend,
But lately he resign'd his breath;
With others I did him attend
Unto the silent house of death.

"For him I wept, for him I mourn'd,
Paid all to friendship that was due;
But sadly friendship is return'd,
Thy Herman he must follow too!

"Young Sigismund, my once dear friend,
But now my persecutor foul,
Doth his malevolence extend
E'en to the torture of my soul.

"From the drear mansion of the tomb,
From the low regions of the dead,
The ghost of Sigismund doth roam,
And dreadful haunts me in my bed!

"There, vested in infernal guise,
(By means to me not understood,)
Close to my side the goblin lies,
And drinks away my vital blood!

"Sucks from my veins the streaming life,
And drains the fountain of my heart!
O Gertrude, Gertrude! dearest wife!
Unutterable is my smart.

"When surfeited, the goblin dire,
With banqueting by suckled gore,
Will to his sepulchre retire,
Till night invites him forth once more.

"Already I'm exhausted, spent;
His carnival is nearly o'er,
My soul with agony is rent,
To-morrow I shall be no more!

"But, O my Gertrude! dearest wife!
The keenest pangs hath last remain'd—
When dead, I too shall seek thy life,
Thy blood by Herman shall be drain'd!

"But to avoid this horrid fate,
Soon as I'm dead and laid in earth,
Drive thro' my corpse a jav'lin straight;—
This shall prevent my coming forth.

"O watch with me, this last sad night,
Watch in your chamber here alone,
But carefully conceal the light
Until you hear my parting groan.

"Then, and just then, thy lamp make bare,
The starting ray, the bursting light,
Shall from my side the goblin scare,
And shew him visible to sight!"

The live-long night poor Gertrude sate,
Watch'd by her sleeping, dying lord;
The live-long night she mourn'd his fate,
The object whom her soul ador'd.

Then at what time the vesper-bell
Of yonder convent sadly toll'd,
Just then was peal'd his passing knell,
The hapless Herman he was cold!

Just at that moment Gertrude drew
From 'neath her cloak the hidden light;
When, dreadful! she beheld in view
The shade of Sigismund!—sad sight!

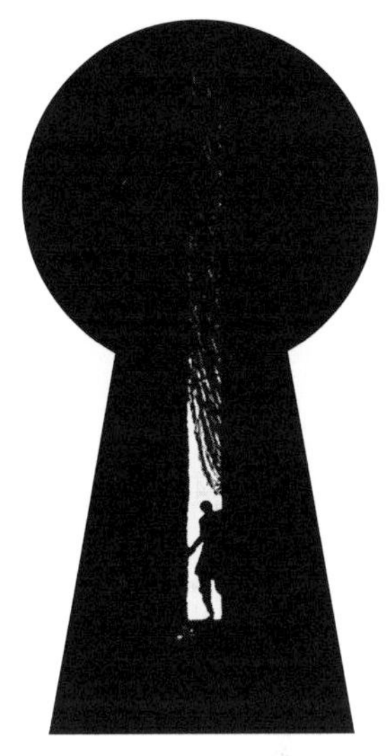

Indignant roll'd his ireful eyes,
That gleam'd with wild horrific stare;
And fix'd a moment with surprise,
Beheld aghast th' enlight'ning glare.

His jaws cadaverous were besmear'd
With clott'd carnage o'er and o'er,
And all his horrid whole appear'd
Distent, and fill'd with human gore!

With hideous scowl the spectre fled;
She shriek'd aloud;—then swoon'd away!
The hapless Herman in his bed,
All pale, a lifeless body lay!

Next day in council 'twas decree,
(Urg'd at the instance of the state,)
That shudd'ring nature should be freed
From pests like these ere 'twas too late.

The choir then burst the fun'ral dome
Where Sigismund was lately laid,
And found him, tho' within the tomb,
Still warm as life, and undecay'd.

With blood his visage was distain'd,
Ensanguin'd were his frightful eyes,
Each sign of former life remain'd,
Save that all motionless he lies.

The corpse of Herman they contrive
To the same sepulchre to take,
And thro' both carcases they drive,
Deep in the earth, a sharpen'd stake!

By this was finish'd their career,
Thro' this no longer they can roam;
From them their friends have nought to fear,
Both quiet keep the slumb'ring tomb.

John Stagg

Dead Man's Hate

They hanged John Farrel in the dawn amid the marketplace;
At dusk came Adam Brand to him and spat upon his face.
"Ho neighbors all," spake Adam Brand, "see ye John Farrel's fate!
"Tis proven here a hempen noose is stronger than man's hate!

For heard ye not John Farrel's vow to be avenged upon me
Come life or death? See how he hangs high on the gallows tree!"
Yet never a word the people spoke, in fear and wild surprise-
For the grisly corpse raised up its head and stared with sightless eyes,

And with strange motions, slow and stiff, pointed at Adam Brand
And clambered down the gibbet tree, the noose within its hand.
With gaping mouth stood Adam Brand like a statue carved of stone,
Till the dead man laid a clammy hand hard on his shoulder bone.

Then Adam shrieked like a soul in hell; the red blood left his face
And he reeled away in a drunken run through the screaming market place;
And close behind, the dead man came with a face like a mummy's mask,
And the dead joints cracked and the stiff legs creaked with their unwonted task.

Men fled before the flying twain or shrank with bated breath,
And they saw on the face of Adam Brand the seal set there by death.
He reeled on buckling legs that failed, yet on and on he fled;
So through the shuddering market-place, the dying fled the dead.

At the riverside fell Adam Brand with a scream that rent the skies;
Across him fell John Farrel's corpse, nor ever the twain did rise.
There was no wound on Adam Brand but his brow was cold and damp,
For the fear of death had blown out his life as a witch blows out a lamp.

His lips were writhed in a horrid grin like a fiend's on Satan's coals,
And the men that looked on his face that day, his stare still haunts their souls.
Such was the fate of Adam Brand, a strange, unearthly fate;
For stronger than death or hempen noose are the fires of a dead man's hate.

Robert Ervin Howard

Oil and Blood

In tombs of gold and lapis lazuli
Bodies of holy men and women exude
Miraculous oil, odour of violet.

But under heavy loads of trampled clay
Lie bodies of the vampires full of blood;
Their shrouds are bloody and their lips are wet.

W. B. Yeats

Hamlet, Act III, Scene II (extract)

'Tis now the very witching time of night,
When churchyards yawn and hell itself breathes out
Contagion to this world: now could I drink hot blood,
And do such bitter business as the day
Would quake to look on.

William Shakespeare

How to Kill

Under the parabola of a ball,
a child turning into a man,
I looked into the air too long.
The ball fell in my hand, it sang
in the closed fist: *Open Open*
Behold a gift designed to kill.

Now in my dial of glass appears
the soldier who is going to die.
He smiles, and moves about in ways
his mother knows, habits of his.
The wires touch his face: I cry
NOW. Death, like a familiar, hears

and look, has made a man of dust
of a man of flesh. This sorcery
I do. Being damned, I am amused
to see the centre of love diffused
and the waves of love travel into vacancy.
How easy it is to make a ghost.

The weightless mosquito touches
her tiny shadow on the stone,
and with how like, how infinite
a lightness, man and shadow meet.
They fuse. A shadow is a man
when the mosquito death approaches.

Keith Douglas

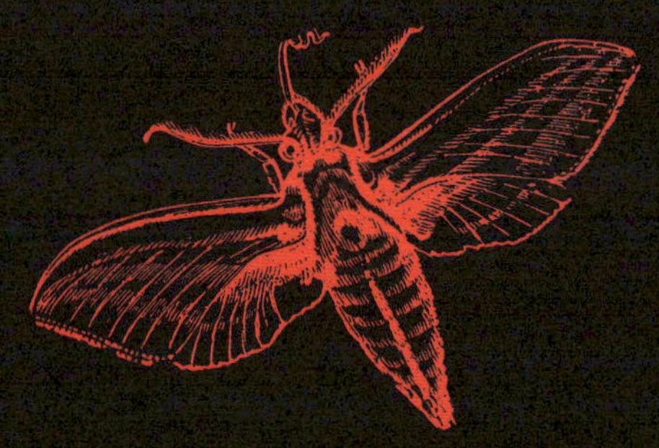

The Laboratory

I

Now that I, tying thy glass mask tightly,
May gaze thro' these faint smokes curling whitely,
As thou pliest thy trade in this devil's-smithy –
Which is the poison to poison her, prithee?

II

He is with her, and they know that I know
Where they are, what they do: they believe my tears flow
While they laugh, laugh at me, at me fled to the drear
Empty church, to pray God in, for them! – I am here.

III

Grind away, moisten and mash up thy paste,
Pound at thy powder, – I am not in haste!
Better sit thus and observe thy strange things,
Than go where men wait me and dance at the King's.

IV

That in the mortar – you call it a gum?
Ah, the brave tree whence such gold oozings come!
And yonder soft phial, the exquisite blue,
Sure to taste sweetly, – is that poison too?

V

Had I but all of them, thee and thy treasures,
What a wild crowd of invisible pleasures!
To carry pure death in an earring, a casket,
A signet, a fan-mount, a filligree basket!

VI

Soon, at the King's, a mere lozenge to give
And Pauline should have just thirty minutes to live!
But to light a pastille, and Elise, with her head
And her breast and her arms and her hands, should drop dead!

VII

Quick – is it finished? The colour's too grim!
Why not soft like the phial's, enticing and dim?
Let it brighten her drink, let her turn it and stir,
And try it and taste, ere she fix and prefer!

VIII

What a drop! She's not little, no minion like me –
That's why she ensnared him: this never will free
The soul from those masculine eyes, – say, "no!"
To that pulse's magnificent come-and-go.

IX

For only last night, as they whispered, I brought
My own eyes to bear on her so, that I thought
Could I keep them one half minute fixed, she would fall,
Shrivelled; she fell not; yet this does not all!

X

Not that I bid you spare her the pain!
Let death be felt and the proof remain;
Brand, burn up, bite into its grace –
He is sure to remember her dying face!

XI

Is it done? Take my mask off! Nay, be not morose
It kills her, and this prevents seeing it close:
The delicate droplet, my whole fortune's fee –
If it hurts her, beside, can it ever hurt me?

XII

Now, take all my jewels, gorge gold to your fill,
You may kiss me, old man, on my mouth if you will!
But brush this dust off me, lest horror it brings
Ere I know it – next moment I dance at the King's!

Robert Browning

A Poison Tree

I was angry with my friend:
I told my wrath, my wrath did end.
I was angry with my foe:
I told it not, my wrath did grow.

And I watered it in fears,
Night & morning with my tears;
And I sunned it with smiles,
And with soft deceitful wiles.

And it grew both day and night,
Till it bore an apple bright.
And my foe beheld it shine,
And he knew that it was mine,

And into my garden stole,
When the night had veild the pole;
In the morning glad I see
My foe outstretched beneath the tree.

William Blake

The Inheritor

Who would have thought the old man had so much blood
So many guts, such yards and yards of guts?
Out of the bucket they trailed in raw festoons
The hungry dog licked at the clammy tubes
And Arnold worked at his un-neat dissection.

Who would have thought one old man went so far?
The sink still gurgled with eternal blood
The bread-bin overflowed its choppered bones
Elusive gristle slithered on the floor
And Arnold dealt with the part that fathered him.

Who would have thought this job would take so long?
For days the copper boiled, the furnace raged
While father billowed forth in obscene smoke
The dog grew sleek with unaccustomed meat
And Arnold at night went on mysterious journeys.

Who would have thought a corpse would cling so hard?
Fragments of father under the finger-nails
Particles in the hair, in the trouser turn-up
But even the skull at last was disposed of secretly
And Arnold lay in the bath content and singing.

Who would have thought this thing would be so simple?
The suit of clothes found on the sea-shore
The empty inquest returning the wished-for verdict
The lawyer discreetly cracking his finger joints
And Arnold in black claiming his heritage.

Geoffrey Parsons

Saturday Market

Bury your heart in some deep green hollow
  Or hide it up in a kind old tree;
Better still, give it the swallow
  When she goes over the sea.

In Saturday's Market there's eggs a 'plenty
  And dead-alive ducks with their legs tied down,
Grey old gaffers and boys of twenty—
  Girls and the women of the town—
Pitchers and sugar-sticks, ribbons and laces,
  Posies and whips and dicky-birds' seed,
Silver pieces and smiling faces,
  In Saturday Market they've all they need.

What were you showing in Saturday Market
  That set it grinning from end to end
Girls and gaffers and boys of twenty—?
  Cover it close with your shawl, my friend—
Hasten you home with the laugh behind you,
  Over the down—, out of sight,
Fasten your door, though no one will find you,
  No one will look on a Market night.

See, you, the shawl is wet, take out from under
  The red dead thing—. In the white of the moon
On the flags does it stir again? Well, and no wonder!
  Best make an end of it; bury it soon.
If there is blood on the hearth who'll know it?
  Or blood on the stairs,
When a murder is over and done why show it?
  In Saturday Market nobody cares.

Then lie you straight on your bed for a short, short weeping
  And still, for a long, long rest,
There's never a one in the town so sure of sleeping
  As you, in the house on the down with a hole in your breast.

  Think no more of the swallow,
    Forget, you, the sea,
Never again remember the deep green hollow
  Or the top of the kind old tree!

Charlotte Mew

The Dole of the King's Daughter

Seven stars in the still water,
And seven in the sky;
Seven sins on the King's daughter,
Deep in her soul to lie.

Red roses are at her feet,
(Roses are red in her red-gold hair)
And O where her bosom and girdle meet
Red roses are hidden there.

Fair is the knight who lieth slain
Amid the rush and reed,
See the lean fishes that are fain
Upon dead men to feed.

Sweet is the page that lieth there,
(Cloth of gold is goodly prey,)
See the black ravens in the air,
Black, O black as the night are they.

What do they there so stark and dead?
(There is blood upon her hand)
Why are the lilies flecked with red?
(There is blood on the river sand.)

There are two that ride from the south and east,
And two from the north and west,
For the black raven a goodly feast,
For the King's daughter rest.

There is one man who loves her true,
(Red, O red, is the stain of gore!)
He hath duggen a grave by the darksome yew,
(One grave will do for four.)

No moon in the still heaven,
In the black water none,
The sins on her soul are seven,
The sin upon his is one.

Oscar Wilde

Porphyria's Lover

The rain set early in tonight,
    The sullen wind was soon awake,
It tore the elm-tops down for spite,
    And did its worst to vex the lake:
    I listened with heart fit to break.
When glided in Porphyria; straight
    She shut the cold out and the storm,
And kneeled and made the cheerless grate
    Blaze up, and all the cottage warm;
    Which done, she rose, and from her form
Withdrew the dripping cloak and shawl,
    And laid her soiled gloves by, untied
Her hat and let the damp hair fall,
    And, last, she sat down by my side
    And called me. When no voice replied,
She put my arm about her waist,
    And made her smooth white shoulder bare,
And all her yellow hair displaced,
    And, stooping, made my cheek lie there,
    And spread, o'er all, her yellow hair,
Murmuring how she loved me—she
    Too weak, for all her heart's endeavor,
To set its struggling passion free
    From pride, and vainer ties dissever,
    And give herself to me forever.
But passion sometimes would prevail,
    Nor could tonight's gay feast restrain
A sudden thought of one so pale
    For love of her, and all in vain:
    So, she was come through wind and rain.
Be sure I looked up at her eyes
    Happy and proud; at last I knew
Porphyria worshipped me; surprise
    Made my heart swell, and still it grew
    While I debated what to do.

That moment she was mine, mine, fair,
    Perfectly pure and good: I found
A thing to do, and all her hair
    In one long yellow string I wound
    Three times her little throat around,
And strangled her. No pain felt she;
    I am quite sure she felt no pain.
As a shut bud that holds a bee,
    I warily oped her lids: again
    Laughed the blue eyes without a stain.
And I untightened next the tress
    About her neck; her cheek once more
Blushed bright beneath my burning kiss:
    I propped her head up as before,
    Only, this time my shoulder bore
Her head, which droops upon it still:
    The smiling rosy little head,
So glad it has its utmost will,
    That all it scorned at once is fled,
    And I, its love, am gained instead!
Porphyria's love: she guessed not how
    Her darling one wish would be heard.
And thus we sit together now,
    And all night long we have not stirred,
    And yet God has not said a word!

Robert Browning

Curse of the Stranglers Wife

Even when he caresses her
gently as the summer night
with crickets chirping
beyond the screen,

how can she not fear
those hands with their
grim muscles and veins?

Bruce Boston

The Leper (extract)

Six months, and now my sweet is dead
  A trouble takes me; I know not
If all were done well, all well said,
  No word or tender deed forgot.

Too sweet, for the least part in her,
  To have shed life out by fragments; yet,
Could the close mouth catch breath and stir,
  I might see something I forget.

Six months, and I still sit and hold
  In two cold palms her cold two feet.
Her hair, half grey half ruined gold,
  Thrills me and burns me in kissing it.

Love bites and stings me through, to see
  Her keen face made of sunken bones.
Her worn-off eyelids madden me,
  That were shot through with purple once.

Algernon Charles Swinburne

Macbeth, Act II, Scene I (extract)

Is this a dagger which I see before me,
The handle toward my hand? Come, let me clutch thee –
I have thee not, and yet I see thee still!
Art thou not, fatal vision, sensible
To feeling as to sight? or art thou but
A dagger of the mind, a false creation,
Proceeding from the heat-oppressèd brain?
I see thee yet, in form as palpable
As this which now I draw.
Thou marshall'st me the way that I was going,
And such an instrument I was to use. –
Mine eyes are made the fools o' the other senses,
Or else worth all the rest. – I see thee still;
And on thy blade and dudgeon, gouts of blood,
Which was not so before. There's no such thing.
It is the bloody business which informs
Thus to mine eyes. Now o'er the one half-world
Nature seems dead, and wicked dreams abuse
The curtained sleep. Witchcraft celebrates
Pale Hecat's offerings; and withered murder,
Alarumed by his sentinel the wolf,
Whose howl's his watch, thus with his stealthy pace,
With Tarquin's ravishing strides, towards his design
Moves like a ghost. Thou sure and firm-set earth,
Hear not my steps, which way they walk, for fear
Thy very stones prate of my whereabout
And take the present horror from the time
Which now suits with it. – Whiles I threat, he lives:
Words to the heat of deeds too cold breath gives.
[*A bell rings*]
I go, and it is done; the bell invites me.
Hear it not, Duncan, for it is a knell
That summons thee to heaven or to hell.

William Shakespeare

Night Song

I hear the night breathing, and the raindrops run
Like the crescent nails of wall-mice after dark's begun;
And the wet wind whispers like a praying nun ...

Shall I kill him? I can do it,
He is such a strengthless fool.
Not a soul will ever know it—

"He was walking by the pool
In the dark, and slipped and drowned there."
There is not a thing to fear—
Yes, I know. But still, at night-time
I'm afraid that I shall hear

The wolf winds snarling, and the raindrops tramp
Like an endless army marching from its black cloud-camp,
And the burnt wick whispering in my old oil-lamp ...

Laura Margaret Haley

each-uisge

here is the moon as a spoon-back. dipped. ready. here is the water. reflected. tea-dark. cup-held. here is the reed-footed bird. lines studied. still. beak held. expectant. here is stirring. under the surface. here the current. the eddy. whirling. folding water. fang-dark. cutting. here is the mane. serpent curved. twisting. here is sclera unhooded. pupils blown. bleeding. into the dark. irises bloated. saturated.

drip

drip

drip

here is the slide. of slick. muscles. chest bared. here is the touch. shiver-spine. here is the pull. the urge. here is the deep. rearing. too close. here am i. spilled milk. seeping. here is the struggle. too late. here is the water. closing. churning. over howling limbs. here is the moon. a witness. grave cold. when has a woman ever been able to change her mind. without punishment.

Karan Chambers

The Sea-Side Cave

"A bird of the air shall carry the voice, and that which hath wings shall tell the matter."

At the dead of night by the side of the Sea
I met my gray-haired enemy,—
The glittering light of his serpent eye
Was all I had to see him by.

At the dead of the night, and stormy weather
We went into a cave together, –
Into a cave by the side of the Sea,
And—he never came out with me!

The flower that up through the April mould
Comes like a miser dragging his gold,
Never made spot of earth so bright
As was the ground in the cave that night.

Dead of night, and stormy weather!
Who should see us going together
Under the black and dripping stone
Of the cave from whence I came alone!

Next day as my boy sat on my knee
He picked the gray hairs off from me,
And told with eyes brimful of fear
How a bird in the meadow near

Over her clay-built nest had spread
Sticks and leaves all bloody red,
Brought from a cave by the side of the Sea
Where some murdered man must be.

Alice Cary

The Sea-Child

Into the world you sent her, mother,
Fashioned her body of coral and foam,
Combed a wave in her hair's warm smother,
And drove her away from home.

In the dark of the night she crept to the town
And under a doorway she laid her down,
The little blue child in the foam-fringed gown.

And never a sister and never a brother
To hear her call, to answer her cry.
Her face shone out from her hair's warm smother
Like a moonkin up in the sky.

She sold her corals; she sold her foam;
Her rainbow heart like a singing shell
Broke in her body: she crept back home.

Peace, go back to the world, my daughter,
Daughter, go back to the darkling land;
There is nothing here but sad sea water,
And a handful of sifting sand.

Katherine Mansfield

The Cruel Mother

She leaned her back unto a thorn,
Three, three, and three by three
And there she has her two babes born.
Three, three, and thirty-three

She took frae 'bout her ribbon-belt,
And there she bound them hand and foot.

She has taen out her wee pen-knife,
And there she ended baith their life.

She has howked a hole baith deep and wide,
She has put them in baith side by side.

She has covered them oer wi a marble stane,
Thinking she would gang maiden hame.

As she was walking by her father's castle wa,
She saw twa pretty babes playing at the ba.

'O bonnie babes, gin ye were mine,
I would dress you up in satin fine.

'O I would dress you in the silk,
And wash you ay in morning milk.'

'O cruel mother, we were thine,
And thou made us to wear the twine.

'O cursed mother, heaven's high,
And that's where thou will neer win nigh.

'O cursed mother, hell is deep,
And there thou'll enter step by step.'

Anonymous (traditional)

Mad Mother

After moonrise in autumn,
By a wandering water,
When a half-muffled moon,
Dazed in a cloudland
Of wandering grey,
Looked pale from the cloud,
Dim branches uncoloured,
In a line with the moon,
Under, over the moon,
Faintly repeated,
A dark woven lacework
In the wan wave . . .
I heard a low singing,
Thin, shadowy singing,
Unwordable woe,
A wail from the ruin
Of a heart desolated,
A mind out of tune,
As a wail from the wind:
A thin faded form by the pale flying moon,
A face with the youth faded out from the eyes,
From the wan, weary eyes,
Save for her not a soul!
Save for her, and a child,
Whom she held by the hand,
In the shadowy silence;
But she ceaseth her singing,
Low saith to the child —
"Come along, dear, with mammy
Under the water,
The soft flying water,
The sheltering water,
The kind, hiding water;
You are going with me!"
Then they went from the shelving
Low shore together
Into the water:

And the child little knew
Where he was going,
Only clung to the mother,
Deeming her wise.
Was she not ever
Wise for her little one,
Love for her little one?
Yea, Love is wise!
Ah! she was true;
But the woes of the world,
Driven home by the devil,
Had maddened her mind,
And the child little knew,
Knew not the mother
Herself little knew,
Even she, even she
Herself little knew!
So they went in together,
Mother and child,
Awaking the cloudland
In the wan water,
Awaking the moon.
"O mammy, how cold it is!"
"Yea, very cold, dear!
Only 'tis colder
Yonder on earth, love,
Yonder on land!"
A gurgle, a silence,
Low wind in the rushes,
Never note more of song now;
Nor mother, nor child knew;
Ah! none of us know!

Roden Berkeley Wriothesley Noel

Sanctuary

This is the bricklayer; hear the thud
Of his heavy load dumped down on stone.
His lustrous bricks are brighter than blood,
His smoking mortar whiter than bone.

Set each sharp-edged, fire-bitten brick
Straight by the plumb-line's shivering length;
Make my marvelous wall so thick
Dead nor living may shake its strength.

Full as a crystal cup with drink
Is my cell with dreams, and quiet, and cool ...
Stop, old man! You must leave a chink;
How can I breathe? *You can't, you fool!*

Elinor Wylie

The Sinner

Why should I sail to new coasts?
Why seek strange lands?
What is there in cliffs that amazes me,
Or in sand that I do not know!

I find no charm in this blue coral sea,
Nor in the coloured sky at nightfall,
All these things I have seen and I remember;
My memories are part of my contaminated self,
The world's beauty rots for me.

God strike me deaf and blind.
Let my flesh close me in as with a wall.
Then cleanse me neither with light nor fire,
But with intimate music, which I cannot hear.

Anna Wickham

Titus Andronicus, Act II, Scene IV (extract)

Speak, gentle niece, what stern ungentle hands
Have lopped and hewed and made thy body bare
Of her two branches, those sweet ornaments,
Whose circling shadows kings have sought to sleep in,
And might not gain so great a happiness
As have thy love? Why dost not speak to me?
Alas, a crimson river of warm blood,
Like to a bubbling fountain stirred with wind,
Doth rise and fall between thy rosèd lips,
Coming and going with thy honey breath.
But, sure, some Tereus hath deflowered thee,
And, lest thou shouldst detect him, cut thy tongue.
Ah, now thou turn'st away thy face for shame,
And notwithstanding all this loss of blood,
As from a conduit with three issuing spouts,
Yet do thy cheeks look red as Titan's face
Blushing to be encountered with a cloud.
Shall I speak for thee? Shall I say 'tis so?
O that I knew thy heart, and knew the beast,
That I might rail at him to ease my mind!
Sorrow concealèd, like an oven stopped,
Doth burn the heart to cinders where it is.
Fair Philomela, she but lost her tongue,
And in a tedious sampler sewed her mind;
But, lovely niece, that mean is cut from thee.
A craftier Tereus, cousin, hast thou met,
And he hath cut those pretty fingers off,
That could have better sewed than Philomel.

William Shakespeare

The Other Side of a Mirror

I sat before my glass one day,
And conjured up a vision bare,
Unlike the aspects glad and gay,
That erst were found reflected there -
The vision of a woman, wild
With more than womanly despair.

Her hair stood back on either side
A face bereft of loveliness.
It had no envy now to hide
What once no man on earth could guess.
It formed the thorny aureole
Of hard, unsanctified distress.

Her lips were open - not a sound
Came though the parted lines of red,
Whate'er it was, the hideous wound
In silence and secret bled.
No sigh relieved her speechless woe,
She had no voice to speak her dread.

And in her lurid eyes there shone
The dying flame of life's desire,
Made mad because its hope was gone,
And kindled at the leaping fire
Of jealousy and fierce revenge,
And strength that could not change nor tire.

Shade of a shadow in the glass,
O set the crystal surface free!
Pass - as the fairer visions pass -
Nor ever more return, to be
The ghost of a distracted hour,
That heard me whisper: - 'I am she!'

Mary Coleridge

One Need Not Be a Chamber

One need not be a Chamber—to be Haunted
One need not be a House—
The Brain has Corridors—surpassing
Material Place—

Far safer, of a Midnight Meeting
External Ghost
Than its interior Confronting—
That Cooler Host.

Far safer, through an Abbey gallop,
The Stones a'chase—
Than Unarmed, one's a'self encounter
In lonesome Place—

Ourself behind ourself, concealed—
Should startle most—
Assassin hid in our Apartment
Be Horror's least.

The Body—borrows a Revolver—
He bolts the Door—
O'erlooking a superior spectre—
Or More—

Emily Dickinson

I Wake and Feel the Fell of Dark, Not Day

I wake and feel the fell of dark, not day.
What hours, O what black hours we have spent
This night! what sights you, heart, saw; ways you went!
And more must, in yet longer light's delay.

With witness I speak this. But where I say
Hours I mean years, mean life. And my lament
Is cries countless, cries like dead letters sent
To dearest him that lives alas! away.

I am gall, I am heartburn. God's most deep decree
Bitter would have me taste: my taste was me;
Bones built in me, flesh filled, blood brimmed the curse.

Selfyeast of spirit a dull dough sours. I see
The lost are like this, and their scourge to be
As I am mine, their sweating selves, but worse.

Gerard Manley Hopkins

In the Desert (extract from *Black Riders and Other Lines*)

III

IN THE DESERT
I SAW A CREATURE, NAKED, BESTIAL,
WHO, SQUATTING UPON THE GROUND,
HELD HIS HEART IN HIS HANDS,
AND ATE OF IT.
I SAID, "IS IT GOOD, FRIEND?"
"IT IS BITTER—BITTER," HE ANSWERED;
"BUT I LIKE IT
BECAUSE IT IS BITTER,
AND BECAUSE IT IS MY HEART."

Stephen Crane

Frenzy

Then was I cast from out my state;
    Two fiends of darkness led my way;
They waked me early, watched me late,
    My dread by night, my plague by day!
Oh! I was made their sport, their play,
    Through many a stormy troubled year;
And how they used their passive prey
    Is sad to tell:—but you shall hear.

Those fiends upon a shaking fen
    Fixed me, in dark tempestuous night;
There never trod the foot of men,
    There flocked the fowl in wintry flight;
There danced the moor's deceitful light
    Above the pool where sedges grow;
And when the morning-sun shone bright,
    It shone upon a field of snow.

They hung me on a bough so small,
    The rook could build her nest no higher;
They fixed me on the trembling ball
    That crowns the steeple's quivering spire;
They set me where the seas retire,
    But drown with their returning tide;
And made me flee the mountain's fire
    When rolling from its burning side.

I've hung upon the ridgy steep
    Of cliffs and held the rambling brier;
I've plunged below the billowy deep,
    Where air was sent me to respire;
I've been where hungry wolves retire;
    And (to complete my woes) I've ran
Where Bedlam's crazy crew conspire
    Against the life of reasoning man.

I've furled in storms the flapping sail,
    By hanging from the topmast-head;
I've served the vilest slaves in jail,
    And picked the dunghill's spoil for bread;
I've made the badger's hole my bed,
    I've wandered with a gipsy crew;
I've dreaded all the guilty dread,
    And done what they would fear to do.

On sand, where ebbs and flows the flood,
    Midway they placed and bade me die;
Propped on my staff, I stoutly stood
    When the swift waves came rolling by;
And high they rose, and still more high,
    Till my lips drank the bitter brine;
I sobbed convulsed, then cast mine eye,
    And saw the tide's re-flowing sign.

And then, my dreams were such as nought
    Could yield but my unhappy case;
I've been of thousand devils caught,
    And thrust into that horrid place,
Where reign dismay, despair, disgrace;
    Furies with iron fangs were there,
To torture that accursed race,
    Doomed to dismay, disgrace, despair.

George Crabbe

No Worst, There Is None. Pitched Past Pitch of Grief

No worst, there is none. Pitched past pitch of grief,
More pangs will, schooled at forepangs, wilder wring.
Comforter, where, where is your comforting?
Mary, mother of us, where is your relief?

My cries heave, herds-long; huddle in a main, a chief-
woe, world-sorrow; on an age-old anvil wince and sing—
Then lull, then leave off. Fury had shrieked "No ling-
ering! Let me be fell: force I must be brief".

O the mind, mind has mountains; cliffs of fall
Frightful, sheer, no-man-fathomed. Hold them cheap
May who ne'er hung there. Nor does long our small
Durance deal with that steep or deep. Here! creep,
Wretch, under a comfort serves in a whirlwind: all
Life death does end and each day dies with sleep.

Gerard Manley Hopkins

Love Rises Up Some Days

Love rises up some days
From a blue couch of light
    Upon the summer sky;
He wakes, and waking plays
With beams and dewdrops white;
His laugh is like the sunniest rain,
    And patters through his voice;
He is so lovely, tolerant, and sane,
    That the heart questions why
It doth not, every hour it beats, rejoice.

Yet sometimes Love awakes
On a black, hellish bed,
    And rises up as hate:
He drinks the hurtful lakes,
He joys to toss and spread
Sparkles of pitchy, rankling flame,
    He joys to play with death;
But when we look on him he is the same
    Quaint child we blest of late,
And every word that once he said he saith.

Michael Field

A Cameo

There was a graven image of Desire
    Painted with red blood on a ground of gold
    Passing between the young men and the old,
And by him Pain, whose body shone like fire,
And Pleasure with gaunt hands that grasped their hire.
    Of his left wrist, with fingers clenched and cold,
    The insatiable Satiety kept hold,
Walking with feet unshod that pashed the mire.
The senses and the sorrows and the sins,
    And the strange loves that suck the breasts of Hate
Till lips and teeth bite in their sharp indenture,
Followed like beasts with flap of wings and fins.
    Death stood aloof behind a gaping grate,
Upon whose lock was written *Peradventure.*

Algernon Charles Swinburne

L'Allegro (extract)

Hence loathèd Melancholy
    Of Cerberus and blackest midnight born,
In Stygian cave forlorn
    'Mongst horrid shapes, and shrieks, and sights unholy,
Find out some uncouth cell,
    Where brooding Darkness spreads his jealous wings,
And the night-raven sings;
    There under ebon shades, and low-browed rocks,
As ragged as thy locks,
    In dark Cimmerian desert ever dwell.

John Milton

The World a Hunt

The World a-hunting is:
The prey poor Man, the Nimrod fierce is Death;
His speedy greyhounds are
Lust, Sickness, Envy, Care,
Strife that ne'er falls amiss,
With all those ills which haunt us while we breathe.
Now if by chance we fly
Of these the eager chase,
Old Age with stealing pace
Casts up his nets, and there we panting die.

William Drummond of Hawthornden

The Shield of War

Lastly, stood War, in glittering arms yclad,
With visage grim, stern looks, and blackly hued;
In his right hand a naked sword he had,
That to the hilts was all with blood imbrued;
And in his left, that kings and kingdoms rued,
Famine and fire he held, and therewithal
He razèd towns and threw down towers and all.

Cities he sacked and realms, that whilom flowered
In honour, glory, and rule above the best,
He overwhelmed and all their fame devoured,
Consumed, destroyed, wasted, and never ceased,
Till he their wealth, their name, and all oppressed;
His face forhewed with wounds, and by his side
There hung his targe, with gashes deep and wide.

Thomas Sackville, Earl of Dorset

The Morrigan Meets a Lover on the Battlefield

We are a black arrow above war, compass west, a slash of moon
and jagged flapping, like a hinged wooden thing hunting wet and red iron
in the rain. *There!* We crow dive and are in the mud, grasping the axe
with your eyes in our mouth. But *soft, soft,* we melt like wax in the lamplight
of your face. Oh, bright one with flickering heart – we dream less prophetic dreams
after we eat. But why are your pockets so full of feathers, why does your woman
wear an oily plume in her coat? Did you know, child, that winged and over water
we're reborn – not once, but twice? Not you. You're already gone. So rise, thief –
it snows on the fells and the wild mare runs like thunder, anger, dread.

Caroline Hardaker

The Masque of Anarchy (extract)

VIII
Last came Anarchy; he rode
On a white horse, splashed with blood;
He was pale even to the lips
Like Death in the Apocalypse.

IX
And he wore a kingly crown;
And in his grasp a sceptre shone;
On his brow this mark I saw –
'I AM GOD, AND KING, AND LAW!'

X
With a pace stately and fast,
Over English land he passed,
Trampling to a mire of blood
The admiring multitude.

XI
And a mighty troop around,
With their trampling shook the ground,
Waving each a bloody sword,
For the service of their Lord.

XII
And with glorious triumph they
Rode through England proud and gay,
Drunk as with intoxication
On the wine of desolation.

XIII
O'er fields and towns, from sea to sea,
Passed the Pageant swift and free,
Tearing up and trampling down
Till they came to London town.

XIV
And each dweller, panic stricken,
Felt his heart with terror sicken
Hearing the tempestuous cry
Of the triumph of Anarchy.

XV
For with pomp to meet him came,
Clothed in arms like blood and flame,
The hired murderers who did sing
'Thou art God and Law and King.

XVI
'We have waited, weak and lone
For thy coming, Mighty One!
Our purses are empty, our swords are cold,
Give us glory, and blood, and gold.'

Percy Bysshe Shelley

I Hear an Army

I hear an army charging upon the land,
    And the thunder of horses plunging, foam about their knees.
Arrogant, in black armour, behind them stand,
    Disdaining the reins, with fluttering whips, the charioteers.

They cry unto the night their battle-name:
    I moan in sleep when I hear afar their whirling laughter.
They cleave the gloom of dreams, a blinding flame,
    Clanging, clanging upon the heart as upon an anvil.

They come shaking in triumph their long, green hair:
    They come out of the sea and run shouting by the shore.
My heart, have you no wisdom thus to despair?
    My love, my love, my love, why have you left me alone?

James Joyce

Black Riders Came From the Sea

(extract from *Black Riders and Other Lines*)

I

BLACK RIDERS CAME FROM THE SEA.
There was clang and clang of spear and shield,
And clash and clash of hoof and heel,
Wild shouts and the wave of hair
In the RUSH upon the wind:
Thus the ride of *sin*.

Stephen Crane

The Dancers

(During a Great Battle, 1916)

The floors are slippery with blood:
The world gyrates too. God is good
That while His wind blows out the light
For those who hourly die for us –
We still can dance, each night.

The music has grown numb with death –
But we will suck their dying breath,
The whispered name they breathed to chance,
To swell our music, make it loud
That we may dance, – may dance.

We are the dull blind carrion-fly
That dance and batten. Though God die
Mad from the horror of the light –
The light is mad, too, flecked with blood, –
We dance, we dance, each night.

Edith Sitwell

To Death

O King of terrors, whose unbounded sway
All that have life must certainly obey;
The King, the Priest, the Prophet, all are thine,
Nor would ev'n God (in flesh) thy stroke decline.
My name is on thy roll, and sure I must
Increase thy gloomy kingdom in the dust.
My soul at this no apprehension feels,
But trembles at thy swords, thy racks, thy wheels;
Thy scorching fevers, which distract the sense,
And snatch us raving, unprepared, from hence;
At thy contagious darts, that wound the heads
Of weeping friends, who wait at dying beds.
Spare these, and let thy time be when it will;
My bus'ness is to die, and thine to kill.
Gently thy fatal scepter on me lay,
And take to thy cold arms, insensibly, thy prey.

Anne Finch, Countess of Winchilsea

The White Horse

What do I stare at—not the colt
That frisks in yon green field; so strong
That he can leap about and run,
Yet is too weak to stand up straight
When his mother licks him with her tongue.

No, no, my eyes go far beyond,
Across that field to yon far hill,
Where one white horse stands there alone;
And nothing else is white to see,
Outside a house all dark and still.

'Death, are you in that house?' think I—
'Is that horse there on your account?
Can I expect a shadow soon,
Seen in that horse's ghostly ribs—
When you come up behind, to mount?'

W. H. Davies

The Unseen

Death went up the hall
Unseen by every one,
Trailing twilight robes
Past the nurse and the nun.
He paused at every door
And listened to the breath
Of those who did not know
How near they were to Death.
Death went up the hall
Unseen by nurse and nun;
He passed by many a door—
But he entered one.

Sara Teasdale

In Time of Pestilence

Adieu, farewell earth's bliss,
This world uncertain is;
Fond are life's lustful joys,
Death proves them all but toys,
None from his darts can fly.
I am sick, I must die.
    Lord, have mercy on us!

Rich men, trust not in wealth,
Gold cannot buy you health;
Physic himself must fade,
All things to end are made.
The plague full swift goes by.
I am sick, I must die.
    Lord, have mercy on us!

Beauty is but a flower
Which wrinkles will devour;
Brightness falls from the air,
Queens have died young and fair,
Dust hath closed Helen's eye.
I am sick, I must die.
    Lord, have mercy on us!

Strength stoops unto the grave,
Worms feed on Hector brave,
Swords may not fight with fate,
Earth still holds ope her gate.
Come! come! the bells do cry.
I am sick, I must die.
    Lord, have mercy on us!

Wit with his wantonness
Tasteth death's bitterness;
Hell's executioner
Hath no ears for to hear
What vain art can reply.
I am sick, I must die.
    Lord, have mercy on us!

Haste, therefore, each degree,
To welcome destiny.
Heaven is our heritage,
Earth but a player's stage;
Mount we unto the sky.
I am sick, I must die;
    Lord, have mercy on us!

Thomas Nashe

Nature's Cook

Death is the cook of nature, and we find
Creatures drest several ways to please her mind;
Some Death doth roast with fevers burning hot,
And some he boils with dropsies in a pot;
Some are consumed for jelly by degrees,
And some with ulcers, gravy out to squeeze;
Some, as with herbs, he stuffs with gouts and pains,
Others for tender meat he hangs in chains;
Some in the sea he pickles up to keep,
Others he, as soused brawn, in wine doth steep;
Some flesh and bones he with the Pox chops small,
And doth a French fricassee make withall;
Some on grid-irons of calentures are broiled,
And some are trodden down, and so quite spoiled:
But some are baked, when smothered they do die,
Some meat he doth by hectick fevers fry;
In sweat sometimes he stews with savoury smell,
An hodge-podge of diseases he likes well;
Some brains he dresseth with apoplexy,
Or fawce of megrims, swimming plenteously;
And tongues he dries with smoak from stomachs ill,
Which, as the second course he sends up still;
Throats he doth cut, blood puddings for to make,
And puts them in the guts, which cholicks rack;
Some hunted are by him for deer, that's red.
And some as stall-fed oxen knocked o'th' head;
Some singed and scald for bacon, seem most rare,
When with salt rheum and phlegm they powdered are.

Margaret Cavendish

Smile, Death

Smile, Death, see I smile as I come to you
    Straight from the road and the moor that I leave behind,
Nothing on earth to me was like this wind-blown space,
Nothing was like the road, but at the end there was a vision or a face
    And the eyes were not always kind.

    Smile, Death, as you fasten the blades to my feet for me,
On, on let us skate past the sleeping willows dusted with snow;
Fast, fast down the frozen stream, with the moor and the road and the vision behind,
    (Show me your face, why the eyes are kind!)
And we will not speak of life or believe in it or remember it as we go.

Charlotte Mew

Lucifer in Starlight

On a starred night Prince Lucifer uprose.
Tired of his dark dominion, swung the fiend
Above the rolling ball in cloud part screened,
Where sinners hugged their specter of repose.
Poor prey to his hot fit of pride were those.
And now upon his western wing he leaned,
Now his huge bulk o'er Afric's sands careened,
Now the black planet shadowed Arctic snows.
Soaring through wider zones that pricked his scars
With memory of the old revolt from Awe,
He reached a middle height, and at the stars,
Which are the brain of heaven, he looked, and sank.
Around the ancient track marched, rank on rank,
The army of unalterable law.

George Meredith

Lucifer Ascending (extract from *The Black Book*)

Now is hell landed here upon the earth,
When Lucifer, in limbs of burning gold,
Ascends this dusty theatre of the world,
To join his powers; and, were it numbered well,
There are more devils of earth than are in hell.
Hence springs my damnèd joy; my tortured spleen
Melts into mirthful humour at this fate,
That heaven is hung so high, drawn up so far,
And made so fast, nailed up with many a star;
And hell the very shop-board of the earth,
Where, when I cut out souls, I throw the shreds
And the white linings of a new soiled spirit,
Pawned to luxurious and adulterous merit.
Yea, that's the sin, and now it takes her turn,
For which the world shall like a strumpet burn;
And for an instance to fire false embraces,
I make the world burn now in secret places;
I haunt invisible corners as a spy,
And in adulterous circles there rise I;
There am I conjured up through hot desire,
And where hell rises, there must needs be fire.
And now that I have vaulted up so high
Above the stage-rails of this earthen globe,
I must turn actor and join companies,
To share my comic sleek-eyed villainies;
For I must weave a thousand ills in one,
To please my black and burnt affection.

Thomas Middleton

De Profundis (extract)

The hecatomb of myriad-fold dumb lives
Invokes a clinging curse on Him who thrives
From their long torture; inarticulate calls
Man's beast progenitor! lo! from hopeless falls
Under the precipice of grand endeavour,
Beautiful youths and maidens, mute for ever,
Piteously silent utter loud reproof
On Him who holds Himself unseen, aloof,
And makes Him sport, engendering their vain
Faith, effort, prayer, the longer to sustain
This miserable mockery of life
Wherewith He endows them, grim and cold, and rife
With cruel humour, with insane, fierce relish
For wine of anguish wrung from tortures hellish
Of souls and bodies! lo! we all pass by,
Saluting Caesar, men who are to die!
Or is it but inevitable, blind
Dull monster Force, that doth terrific grind
Forth idle aspiration, and fond fears,
Illusive bliss, and terror, and wild tears
From one dim, boundless chaos of a womb,
Till, white with horror of the waking doom,
All cower for refuge in their natal tomb?

Roden Berkeley Wriothesley Noel

Paradise Lost (Book 2, extract)

Before the gates there sat
On either side a formidable shape;
The one seemed woman to the waste, and fair,
But ended foul in many a scaly fold
Voluminous and vast, a serpent armed
With mortal sting. About her middle round
A cry of Hellhounds never ceasing barked
With wide Cerberean mouths full loud, and rung
A hideous peal: yet, when they list, would creep,
If aught disturbed their noise, into her womb,
And kennel there, yet there still barked and howled
Within unseen. Far less abhorred than these
Vexed Scylla, bathing in the sea that parts
Calabria from the hoarse Trinacrian shore:
Nor uglier follow the night-hag, when called
In secret, riding through the air she comes,
Lured with the smell of infant blood, to dance
With Lapland witches, while the labouring moon
Eclipses at their charms. The other shape,
If shape it might be called that shape had none
Distinguishable in member, joint, or limb,
Or substance might be called that shadow seemed,
For each seemed either; black it stood as night,
Fierce as ten Furies, terrible as Hell,
And shook a dreadful dart; what seemed his head
The likeness of a kingly crown had on.

John Milton

Chapter Two

Hauntings

"Up we ride from the dim places"

'Call of the Dead', Anna Wickham

Woman Death

Wash over her, wet light
Of this dissolving room.
Dusk smelling of night,
Lay on her placid gloom.
Wash over her; as waves push back the sands
Fold down her hands.

Many another rain
Of dusk has filled such walls;
Many a woman has lain
Submerged where the damp light falls,
Wanting her hands held down,
Finding it strange that they
Alone refuse to drown.

The mind after its day
Fills like an iron cup
With waters of the night.
The eyes wisely give up
The little they held of light.
Move over her, subdue her, Dark, until
Her hands are still.

Out of the east comes night;
From west, from north, from south,
Gathers the blackened light
To move against her mouth.
Many another has known
These four pressures of space,
Feeling her lips grow stone

And hollows curving her face,
And cared so little to feel.
Her light had never given
More than her dark might steal;
Then for this she had striven:
To feel the quiet moving on her hands
Like thin sea over sands.

Time gathers to break
In arrested thunder, gloom
Comes with thickness to make
Deep ocean of a room,
Comes to soothe and shape
The breathed-out breath.

Some who die escape
The rhythm of their death,
Some may die and know
Death as a broken song,
But a woman dies not so, not so;
A woman's death is long.

Hazel Hall

Following

So she follows the trail of her father's coat through the fair
Shouldering past beasts packed solid as books,
And the dealing men nearly as slow to give way –
A block of a belly, a back like a mountain,
A shifting elbow like a plumber's bend –
When she catches a glimpse of a shirt-cuff, a handkerchief,
Then the hard brim of his hat, skimming along,

Until she is tracing light footsteps
Across the shivering bog by starlight,
The dead corpse risen from the wakehouse
Gliding before her in a white habit.
The ground is forested with gesturing trunks,
Hands of women dragging needles,
Half-choked heads in the water of cuttings,
Mouths that roar like the noise of the fair day.

She comes to where he is seated
With whiskey poured out in two glasses
In a library where the light is clean,
His clothes all finely laundered,
Ironed facings and linings.
The smooth foxed leaf has been hidden
In a forest of fine shufflings,
The square of white linen
That held three drops
Of her heart's blood is shelved
Between the gatherings
That go to make a book –
The crushed flowers among the pages crack
The spine open, push the bindings apart.

Eiléan Ní Chuilleanáin

Beautiful Girls

In our graves we are all
beautiful girls. Our skin
is falling away like the tide.
Our bones are
long and slender,
all inhibitions gone. We're
lovely in the mud
that fit boys have dug
for a council wage,
not knowing how beautiful
we lay there
like honeymoon brides
anticipating sex,
not expecting death –
serene as pawns and queens
and home in ourselves
forever.

Melissa Lee-Houghton

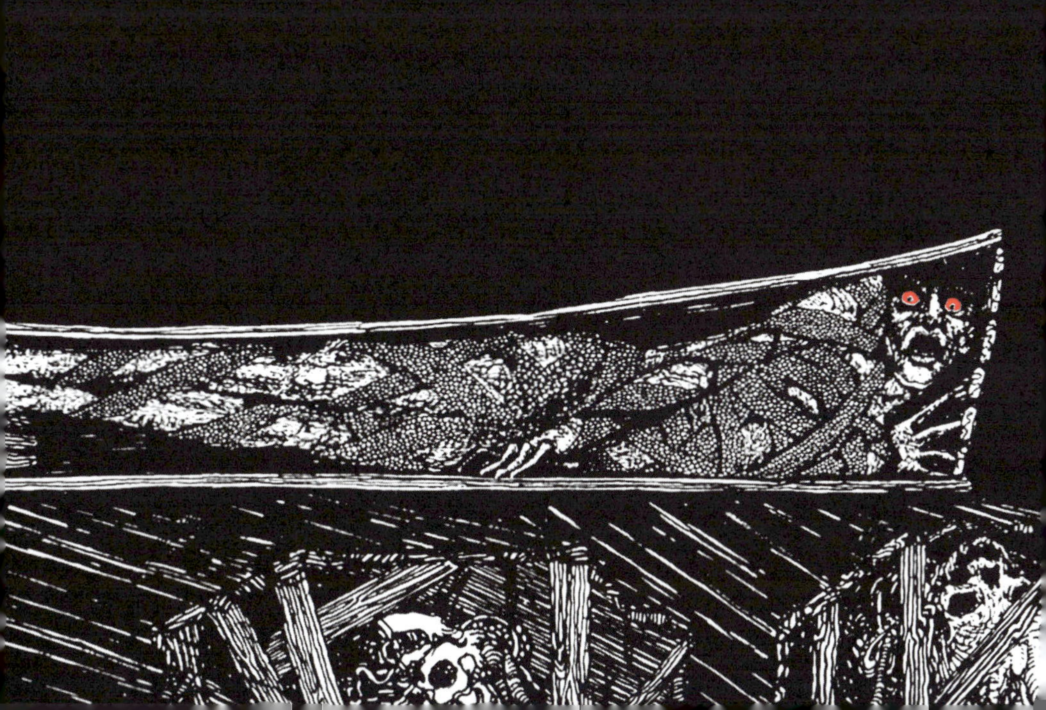

Nature, That Washed Her Hands in Milk

Nature, that washed her hands in milk,
And had forgot to dry them,
Instead of earth took snow and silk,
At love's request to try them,
If she a mistress could compose
To please love's fancy out of those.

Her eyes he would should be of light,
A violet breath, and lips of jelly;
Her hair not black, nor overbright,
And of the softest down her belly;
As for her inside he'd have it
Only of wantonness and wit.

At love's entreaty such a one
Nature made, but with her beauty
She hath framed a heart of stone;
So as love, by ill destiny,
Must die for her whom nature gave him,
Because her darling would not save him.

But time (which nature doth despise,
And rudely gives her love the lie,
Makes hope a fool, and sorrow wise)
His hands do neither wash nor dry;
But being made of steel and rust,
Turns snow and silk and milk to dust.

The light, the belly, lips, and breath,
He dims, discolors, and destroys;
With those he feeds but fills not death,
Which sometimes were the food of joys.
Yea, time doth dull each lively wit,
And dries all wantonness with it.

Oh, cruel time! which takes in trust
Our youth, our joys, and all we have,
And pays us but with age and dust;
Who in the dark and silent grave
When we have wandered all our ways
Shuts up the story of our days.

Sir Walter Raleigh

Pallor

The great white lilies in the grass
    Are pallid as the smile of death;
For they remember still – alas! –
    The graves they sprang from underneath.

The angels up in heaven are pale –
    For all have died, when all is said;
Nor shall the lutes of Eden avail
    To let them dream they are not dead.

Agnes Mary Frances Robinson

The Ghost

I wish you'd a farm on the hills, my Dear,
And need not work for hire.
For though I'm cold in the churchyard here,
And cannot sit by your fire,
I'd walk the paths of your house, some nights,
And haply look into your room:
Then I'd always see my Love's home-lights
When I stood on the rail of my tomb.

Anna Wickham

Barbara

On the Sabbath-day,
Through the churchyard old and gray,
Over the crisp and yellow leaves I held my rustling way;
And amid the words of mercy, falling on my soul like balms,
'Mid the gorgeous storms of music—in the mellow organ-calms,
'Mid the upward-streaming prayers, and the rich and solemn psalms,
I stood careless, Barbara.

My heart was otherwhere,
While the organ shook the air,
And the priest, with outspread hands, bless'd the people with a prayer;
But when rising to go homeward, with a mild and saintlike shine
Gleam'd a face of airy beauty with its heavenly eyes on mine —
Gleam'd and vanish'd in a moment — O that face was surely thine
Out of heaven, Barbara!

O pallid, pallid face!
O earnest eyes of grace!
When last I saw thee, dearest, it was in another place.
You came running forth to meet me with my love-gift on your wrist:
The flutter of a long white dress, then all was lost in mist —
A purple stain of agony was on the mouth I kiss'd,
That wild morning, Barbara.

I search'd, in my despair,
Sunny noon and midnight air;
I could not drive away the thought that you were lingering there.
O many and many a winter night I sat when you were gone,
My worn face buried in my hands, beside the fire alone —
Within the dripping churchyard, the rain plashing on your stone,
You were sleeping, Barbara.

'Mong angels, do you think
Of the precious golden link
I clasp'd around your happy arm while sitting by yon brink?
Or when that night of gliding dance, of laughter and guitars,
Was emptied of its music, and we watch'd, through lattice-bars,
The silent midnight heaven creeping o'er us with its stars,
Till the day broke, Barbara?

In the years I've changed;
Wild and far my heart has ranged,
And many sins and errors now have been on me avenged;
But to you I have been faithful whatsoever good I lack'd:
I loved you, and above my life still hangs that love intact —
Your love the trembling rainbow, I the reckless cataract.
Still I love you, Barbara.

Yet, Love, I am unblest;
With many doubts opprest,
I wander like the desert wind without a place of rest.
Could I but win you for an hour from off that starry shore,
The hunger of my soul were still'd; for Death hath told you more
Than the melancholy world doth know — things deeper than all lore
You could teach me, Barbara.

In vain, in vain, in vain!
You will never come again.
There droops upon the dreary hills a mournful fringe of rain;
The gloaming closes slowly round, loud winds are in the tree,
Round selfish shores for ever moans the hurt and wounded sea;
There is no rest upon the earth, peace is with Death and thee —
Barbara!

Alexander Smith

The Terrible Door

Too long outside your door I have shivered.
You open it? I WILL NOT STAY.
I'm haunted by your ashen beauty.
Take back your hand. I have gone away.

Don't talk, but move to that near corner.
I loathe the long cold shadow here.
We will stand a moment in the lamplight,
Until I watch you HARD and NEAR.

Happy release! Good-bye for ever!
Here at the corner we say good-bye.
But if you want me, if you do need me,
Who waits, at the terrible door, BUT I?

Harold Monro

Hallowe'en

It was down in the woodland on last Hallowe'en,
Where silence and darkness had built them a lair,
That I felt the dim presence of her, the unseen,
And heard her still step on the hush-haunted air.

It was last Hallowe'en in the glimmer and swoon
Of mist and of moonlight, where once we had sinned,
That I saw the gray gleam of her eyes in the moon,
And hair, like a raven, blown wild on the wind.

It was last Hallowe'en where starlight and dew
Made mystical marriage on flower and leaf,
That she led me with looks of a love, that I knew
Was dead, and the voice of a passion too brief.

It was last Hallowe'en in the forest of dreams,
Where trees are eidolons and flowers have eyes,
That I saw her pale face like the foam of far streams,
And heard, like the night-wind, her tears and her sighs.

It was last Hallowe'en, the haunted, the dread,
In the wind-tattered wood, by the storm-twisted pine,
That I, who am living, kept tryst with the dead,
And clasped her a moment who once had been mine.

Madison Cawein

True Love

Farewell, Earl Richard,
Tender and brave;
Kneeling I kiss
The dust from thy grave.

Pray for me, Richard,
Lying alone,
With hands pleading earnestly,
All in white stone.

Soon must I leave thee
This sweet summer tide;
That other is waiting
To claim his pale bride.

Soon I'll return to thee,
Hopeful and brave,
When the dead leaves
Blow over thy grave.

Then shall they find me
Close at thy head,
Watching or fainting,
Sleeping or dead.

Elizabeth Siddal

The Bride

My love looks like a girl tonight,
    But she is old.
The plaits that lie along her pillow
    Are not gold,
But threaded with filigree silver,
    And uncanny cold.

She looks like a young maiden, since her brow
    Is smooth and fair;
Her cheeks are very smooth, her eyes are closed,
    She sleeps a rare,
Still, winsome sleep, so still, and so composed.

Nay, but she sleeps like a bride, and dreams her dreams
    Of perfect things.
She lies at last, the darling, in the shape of her dream,
    And her dead mouth sings
By its shape, like thrushes in clear evenings.

D. H. Lawrence

Embalmment

Let not a star suspect the mystery!
A cave that haunts thee in the dreams of night
Keep me as treasure hidden from thy sight,
And only thine while thou dost covet me!
As the Asmonaean queen perpetually
Embalmed in honey, cold to thy delight,
Cold to thy touch, a sleeping eremite,
Beside thee never sleeping I would be.

Or thou might'st lay me in a sepulchre,
And every line of life will keep its bloom,
Long as thou seal'st me from the common air.
Speak not, reveal not ...   There will be
In the unchallenged dark a mystery,
And golden hair sprung rapid in a tomb.

Michael Field

The Dead Friend (extract)

II

The house was empty where you came no more;
I sat in awe and dread;
When, lo! I heard a hand that shook the door,
And knew it was the Dead.

One moment – ah! – the anguish took my side,
The fainting of the will.
'God of the living, leave me not!' I cried,
And all my flesh grew chill.

One moment; then I opened wide my heart
And open flung the door:
'What matter whence thou comest, what thou art? –
Come to me!" ... Nevermore.

Agnes Mary Frances Robinson

Fragment of a Ballad

Many a mile over land and sea
Unsummoned my love returned to me;
I remember not the words he said
But only the trees moaning overhead.

And he came ready to take and bear
The cross I had carried for many a year,
But words came slowly one by one
From frozen lips shut still and dumb.

How sounded my words so still and slow
To the great strong heart that loved me so,
Who came to save me from pain and wrong
And to comfort me with his love so strong?

I felt the wind strike chill and cold
And vapours rise from the red-brown mould;
I felt the spell that held my breath
Bending me down to a living death.

Elizabeth Siddal

The Unquiet Grave

"The wind doth blow today, my love,
And a few small drops of rain;
I never had but one true-love,
In cold grave she was lain.

"I'll do as much for my true-love
As any young man may;
I'll sit and mourn all at her grave
For a twelvemonth and a day."

The twelvemonth and a day being up,
The dead began to speak:
"Oh who sits weeping on my grave,
And will not let me sleep?"

"'Tis I, my love, sits on your grave,
And will not let you sleep;
For I crave one kiss of your clay-cold lips,
And that is all I seek."

"You crave one kiss of my clay-cold lips,
But my breath smells earthy strong;
If you have one kiss of my clay-cold lips,
Your time will not be long.

"'Tis down in yonder garden green,
Love, where we used to walk,
The finest flower that e're was seen
Is withered to a stalk.

"The stalk is withered dry, my love,
So will our hearts decay;
So make yourself content, my love,
Till God calls you away."

Anonymous

The Poor Ghost

'Oh whence do you come, my dear friend, to me,
With your golden hair all fallen below your knee,
And your face as white as snowdrops on the lea,
And your voice as hollow as the hollow sea?'

'From the other world I come back to you:
My locks are uncurled with dripping drenching dew,
You know the old, whilst I know the new:
But to-morrow you shall know this too.'

'Oh not to-morrow into the dark, I pray;
Oh not to-morrow, too soon to go away:
Here I feel warm and well-content and gay:
Give me another year, another day.'

'Am I so changed in a day and a night
That mine own only love shrinks from me with fright,
Is fain to turn away to left or right
And cover up his eyes from the sight?'

'Indeed I loved you, my chosen friend,
I loved you for life, but life has an end;
Through sickness I was ready to tend:
But death mars all, which we cannot mend.

'Indeed I loved you; I love you yet,
If you will stay where your bed is set,
Where I have planted a violet,
Which the wind waves, which the dew makes wet.'

'Life is gone, then love too is gone,
It was a reed that I leant upon:
Never doubt I will leave you alone
And not wake you rattling bone with bone.

'I go home alone to my bed,
Dug deep at the foot and deep at the head,
Roofed in with a load of lead,
Warm enough for the forgotten dead.

'But why did your tears soak through the clay,
And why did your sobs wake me where I lay?
I was away, far enough away:
Let me sleep now till the Judgment Day.'

Christina Rossetti

Call of the Dead

The stone is riven, I'm free, I'm free.
Come out, my Ransomer, out to me.
Leave the wrecked tenement behind;
The night is ours, and the night wind.
Up we ride from the dim places,
Out we swim through the great spaces,
Driven in tracks of liberty
On ether-piercing ecstasy.
Follow me quick, my Love, my Friend,
To the blue steep at Time's end.

Anna Wickham

Dirge

We do lie beneath the grass
    In the moonlight, in the shade
Of the yew-tree. They that pass
    Hear us not. We are afraid
        They would envy our delight,
        In our graves by glow-worm night.
Come follow us, and smile as we;
    We sail to the rock in the ancient waves,
Where the snow falls by thousands into the sea,
    And the drown'd and the shipwreck'd have happy graves.

Thomas Lovell Beddoes

Epitaph

The first time I died, I walked my ways;
I followed the file of limping days.

I held me tall, with my head flung up,
But I dared not look on the new moon's cup.

I dared not look on the sweet young rain,
And between my ribs was a gleaming pain.

The next time I died, they laid me deep.
They spoke worn words to hallow my sleep.

They tossed me petals, they wreathed me fern,
They weighted me down with a marble urn.

And I lie here warm, and I lie here dry,
And watch the worms slip by, slip by.

Dorothy Parker

Hallowe'en (extract)

The ghosts of all things, past parade,
Emerging from the mist and shade
That hid them from our gaze,
And full of song and ringing mirth,
In one glad moment of rebirth,
Again they walk the ways of earth,
As in the ancient days.

The beacon light shines on the hill,
The will-o'-wisps the forests fill
With flashes filched from noon;
And witches on their broomsticks spry
Speed here and yonder in the sky,
And lift their strident voices high
Unto the Hunter's moon.

The air resounds with tuneful notes
From myriads of straining throats,
All hailing Folly Queen;
So join the swelling choral throng,
Forget your sorrow and your wrong,
In one glad hour of joyous song
To honor Hallowe'en.

John Kendrick Bangs

All Souls'

I

A thin moon faints in the sky o'erhead,
And dumb in the churchyard lie the dead.
Walk we not, Sweet, by garden ways,
Where the late rose hangs and the phlox delays,
But forth of the gate and down the road,
Past the church and the yews, to their dim abode.
For it's turn of the year and All Souls' night,
When the dead can hear and the dead have sight.

II

Fear not that sound like wind in the trees:
It is only their call that comes on the breeze;
Fear not the shudder that seems to pass:
It is only the tread of their feet on the grass;
Fear not the drip of the bough as you stoop:
It is only the touch of their hands that grope –
For the year's on the turn, and it's All Souls' night,
When the dead can yearn and the dead can smite.

III

And where should a man bring his sweet to woo
But here, where such hundreds were lovers too?
Where lie the dead lips that thirst to kiss,
The empty hands that their fellows miss,
Where the maid and her lover, from sere to green,
Sleep bed by bed, with the worm between?
For it's turn of the year and All Souls' night,
When the dead can hear and the dead have sight.

IV

And now that they rise and walk in the cold,
Let us warm their blood and give youth to the old.
Let them see us and hear us, and say: 'Ah, thus
In the prime of the year it went with us!'
Till their lips drawn close, and so long unkist,
Forget they are mist that mingles with mist!
For the year's on the turn, and it's All Souls' night,
When the dead can burn and the dead can smite.

V

Till they say, as they hear us – poor dead, poor dead! –
'Just an hour of this, and our age-long bed –
Just a thrill of the old remembered pains
To kindle a flame in our frozen veins,
Just a touch, and a sight, and a floating apart,
As the chill of dawn strikes each phantom heart –
For it's turn of the year and All Souls' night,
When the dead can hear, and the dead have sight.'

VI

And where should the living feel alive
But here in this wan white humming hive,
As the moon wastes down, and the dawn turns cold,
And one by one they creep back to the fold?
And where should a man hold his mate and say:
'One more, one more, ere we go their way'?
For the year's on the turn, and it's All Souls' night,
When the living can learn by the churchyard light.

VII

And how should we break faith who have seen
Those dead lips plight with the mist between,
And how forget, who have seen how soon
They lie thus chambered and cold to the moon?
How scorn, how hate, how strive, we too,
Who must do so soon as those others do?
For it's All Souls' night, and break of the day,
And behold, with the light the dead are away ...

Edith Wharton

Lenore (extract)

See, see, see! by the gallows-tree,
As they dance on the wheels' broad hoop,
Up and down in the gleam of the moon
Half lost, an airy group:—
"Ho! ho! mad mob, come hither amain,
And join in the wake of my rushing train;—
Come, dance me a dance, ye dancers thin.
Ere the planks of the marriage-bed close us in."

But see! but see! in an eyelid's beat,
Towhoo! a ghastly wonder!
The horseman's jerkin, piece by piece,
Dropped off like brittle tinder!
Fleshless and hairless, a naked skull,
The sight of his weird head was horrible;
The lifelike mask was there no more,
And a scythe and a sandglass the skeleton bore.

Loud snorted the horse as he plunged and reared,
And the sparks were scattered round:—
What man shall say if he vanished away,
Or sank in the gaping ground?
Groans from the earth and shrieks in the air!
Howling and wailing everywhere!
Half dead, half living, the soul of Lenore
Fought as it never had fought before.

The churchyard troop,— a ghostly group,—
Close round the dying girl;
Out and in they hurry and spin
Through the dance's weary whirl:
"Patience, patience, when the heart is breaking;
With thy God there is no question-making:
Of thy body thou art quit and free:
Heaven keep thy soul eternally!"

Gottfried August Bürger
(trans. Dante Gabriel Rossetti)

The Skeleton in the Cupboard

Just this one day in all the year
Let all be one, let all be dear;
Wife, husband, child in fond embrace,
And thrust the phantom from its place.
No bitter words, no frowning brow,
Disturb the Christmas festal, now
The skeleton's behind the door.

Nor let the child, with looks askance,
Find out its sad inheritance
From souls that held no happiness,
Of home, where love is seldom guest;
But in his coming years retain
This one sweet night that had no pain;
The skeleton's behind the door.

In vain you raise the wassail bowl,
And pledge your passion, soul to soul
You hear the sweet bells ring in rhyme,
You wreath the room for Christmas-time
In vain. The solemn silence falls,
The death-watch ticks within the walls;
The skeleton taps on the door.
Then let him back into his place,
Let us sit out the old disgrace;
Nor seek the phantom now to lay
That haunted us through every day;
For plainer is the ghost; useless
Is this pretence of happiness;
The skeleton taps on the door.

Dora Sigerson Shorter

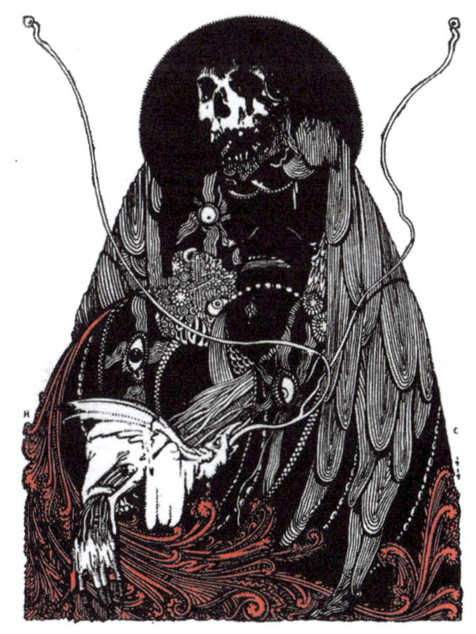

On the Threshold

O God, my dream! I dreamed that you were dead;
Your mother hung above the couch and wept
Whereon you lay all white, and garlanded
With blooms of waxen whiteness. I had crept
Up to your chamber-door, which stood ajar,
And in the doorway watched you from afar,
Nor dared advance to kiss your lips and brow.
I had no part nor lot in you, as now;
Death had not broken between us the old bar;
Nor torn from out my heart the old, cold sense
Of your misprision and my impotence.

Amy Levy

The Ghosts' Moonshine

It is midnight, my wedded;
Let us lie under
The tempest bright undreaded,
In the warm thunder:
(Tremble and weep not! What can you fear?)
My heart's best wish is thine, –
That thou wert white, and bedded
On the softest bier,
In the ghosts' moonshine.
Is that the wind? No, no;
Only two devils, that blow
Through the murderer's ribs to and fro,
In the ghosts' moonshine.
Who is there, she said afraid, yet
Stirring and awaking
The poor old dead? His spade, it
Is only making, –
(Tremble and weep not! What do you crave?)
Where yonder grasses twine,
A pleasant bed, my maid, that
Children call a grave,
In the cold moonshine.
Is that the wind? No, no;
Only two devils, that blow
Through the murderer's ribs to and fro,
In the ghosts' moonshine.
What dost thou strain above her
Lovely throat's whiteness?
A silken Chain, to cover
Her bosom's brightness?
(Tremble and weep not: what dost thou fear?)
– My blood is spilt like wine,
Thou hast strangled and slain me, lover,
Thou hast stabbed me dear,
In the ghosts' moonshine.
Is that the wind? No, no;
Only her goblin doth blow
Through the murderer's ribs to and fro,
In its own moonshine.

Thomas Lovell Beddoes

William and Margaret

'Twas at the silent, solemn hour,
When night and morning meet;
In glided Margaret's grimly ghost,
And stood at William's feet.

Her face was like an April morn,
Clad in a wintry cloud:
And clay-cold was her lily-hand,
That held her sable shroud.

So shall the fairest face appear,
When youth and years are flown:
Such is the robe that kings must wear,
When death has reft their crown.

Her bloom was like the springing flower,
That sips the silver dew;
The rose was budded in her cheek,
Just opening to the view.

But love had, like the canker-worm,
Consumed her early prime:
The rose grew pale, and left her cheek;
She died before her time.

'Awake!' she cried, 'thy true love calls,
Come from her midnight grave;
Now let thy pity hear the maid
Thy love refused to save.

'This is the dumb and dreary hour,
When injured ghosts complain;
When yawning graves give up their dead,
To haunt the faithless swain.

'Bethink thee, William, of thy fault,
Thy pledge and broken oath:
And give me back my maiden vow,
And give me back my troth.

'Why did you promise love to me,
And not that promise keep?
Why did you swear my eyes were bright,
Yet leave those eyes to weep?

'How could you say my face was fair,
    And yet that face forsake?
How could you win my virgin heart,
    Yet leave that heart to break?

'Why did you say my lip was sweet,
    And made the scarlet pale?
And why did I, young witless maid,
    Believe the flattering tale!

'That face, alas! no more is fair;
    Those lips no longer red:
Dark are my eyes, now closed in death,
    And every charm is fled.

'The hungry worm my sister is;
    This winding sheet I wear:
And cold and weary lasts our night,
    Till that last morn appear.

'But hark!—the cock has warned me hence;
    A long and late adieu!
Come, see, false man, how low she lies,
    Who died for love of you.'

The lark sung loud; the morning smiled,
    And raised her glistering head;
Pale William quaked in every limb,
    And raving left his bed.

He hied him to the fatal place
    Where Margaret's body lay:
And stretched him on the grass-green turf,
    That wrapped her breathless clay.

And thrice he called on Margaret's name,
    And thrice he wept full sore:
Then laid his cheek to her cold grave,
    And word spake never more.

David Mallet

The Drowned Mariner

A mariner sat on the shrouds one night,
The wind was piping free;
Now bright, now dimmed was the moonlight pale,
And the phosphor gleamed in the wake of the whale,
As he floundered in the sea;
The scud was flying athwart the sky,
The gathering winds went whistling by,
And the wave as it towered, then fell in spray,
Looked an emerald wall in the moonlight ray.

The mariner swayed and rocked on the mast,
But the tumult pleased him well;
Down the yawning wave his eye he cast,
And the monsters watched as they hurried past
Or lightly rose and fell;
For their broad, damp fins were under the tide,
And they lashed as they passed the vessel's side,
And their filmy eyes, all huge and grim,
Glared fiercely up, and they glared at him.

Now freshens the gale, and the brave ship goes
Like an uncurbed steed along;
A sheet of flame is the spray she throws,
As her gallant prow the water ploughs,
But the ship is fleet and strong:
The topsails are reefed and the sails are furled,
And onward she sweeps o'er the watery world,
And dippeth her spars in the surging flood;
But there came no chill to the mariner's blood.

Wildly she rocks, but he swingeth at ease,
And holds him by the shroud;
And as she careens to the crowding breeze,
The gaping deep the mariner sees,
And the surging heareth loud.
Was that a face, looking up at him,
With its pallid cheek and its cold eyes dim?
Did it beckon him down? did it call his name?
Now rolleth the ship the way whence it came.

The mariner looked, and he saw with dread
A face he knew too well;
And the cold eyes glared, the eyes of the dead,
And its long hair out on the wave was spread.
Was there a tale to tell?

The stout ship rocked with a reeling speed,
And the mariner groaned, as well he need;
For, ever, down as she plunged on her side,
The dead face gleamed from the briny tide.

Bethink thee, mariner, well, of the past, —
  A voice calls loud for thee: —
There 's a stifled prayer, the first, the last; —
The plunging ship on her beam is cast, —
  Oh, where shall thy burial be?
Bethink thee of oaths that were lightly spoken,
Bethink thee of vows that were lightly broken,
Bethink thee of all that is dear to thee,
For thou art alone on the raging sea:

Alone in the dark, alone on the wave,
  To buffet the storm alone,
To struggle aghast at thy watery grave,
To struggle and feel there is none to save, —
  God shield thee, helpless one!
The stout limbs yield, for their strength is past,
The trembling hands on the deep are cast,
The white brow gleams a moment more,
Then slowly sinks—the struggle is o'er.

Down, down where the storm is hushed to sleep,
  Where the sea its dirge shall swell,
Where the amber drops for thee shall weep,
And the rose-lipped shell her music keep,
  There thou shalt slumber well.
The gem and the pearl lie heaped at thy side,
They fell from the neck of the beautiful bride,
From the strong man's hand, from the maiden's brow,
As they slowly sunk to the wave below.

A peopled home is the ocean bed;
  The mother and child are there;
The fervent youth and the hoary head,
The maid, with her floating locks outspread,
  The babe with its silken hair;
As the water moveth they lightly sway,
And the tranquil lights on their features play;
And there is each cherished and beautiful form,
Away from decay, and away from the storm.

Elizabeth Oakes Smith

He Wishes His Beloved Were Dead

Were you but lying COLD and DEAD,
And lights were *paling* out of the West,
You would COME HITHER, and bend your head,
And I would *lay my head* on your breast;
And you would MURMUR tender words,
Forgiving me, because you were D E A D :
Nor would you *rise* and hasten away,
Though you have THE WILL of the wild birds,
But know your hair was ***bound*** and ***wound***
About the STARS and MOON and SUN:
O would, *beloved*, that you lay
U N D E R the dock-leaves in the ground,
While lights were paling ***one by one***.

W. B. Yeats

The Apparition

When by thy scorn, O murd'ress, I am dead,
    And that thou thinkst thee free
From all solicitation from me,
Then shall my ghost come to thy bed,
And thee, fained vestal, in worse arms shall see;
Then thy sick taper will begin to wink,
And he, whose thou art then, being tired before,
Will, if thou stir, or pinch to wake him, think
    Thou call'st for more,
And in false sleep will from thee shrink,
And then, poor aspen wretch, neglected thou
Bathed in a cold quicksilver sweat wilt lie,
    A verier ghost than I;
What I will say, I will not tell thee now,
Lest that preserve thee; and since my love is spent,
I had rather thou shouldst painfully repent,
Than by my threatnings rest still innocent.

John Donne

When Thou Must Home

When thou must home to shades of underground,
    And there arrived, a new admirèd guest,
The beauteous spirits do engirt thee round,
    White Iope, blithe Helen, and the rest,
To hear the stories of thy finished love
From that smooth tongue, whose music hell can move:

Then wilt thou speak of banqueting delights,
    Of masks and revels which sweet youth did make,
Of tourneys and great challenges of knights,
    And all these triumphs for thy beauty's sake:
When thou hast told these honours done to thee,
Then tell, oh! tell, how thou didst murder me.

Thomas Campion

The Inquest

I took my oath I would inquire,
    Without affection, hate, or wrath,
Into the death of Ada Wright –
    So help me God! I took that oath.

When I went out to see the corpse,
    The four months' babe that died so young,
I judged it was seven pounds in weight,
    And little more than one foot long.

One eye, that had a yellow lid,
    Was shut – so was the mouth, that smiled;
The left eye open, shining bright –
    It seemed a knowing little child.

For as I looked at that one eye,
    It seemed to laugh, and say with glee:
'What caused my death you'll never know –
    Perhaps my mother murdered me.'

When I went into court again,
    To hear the mother's evidence –
It was a love-child, she explained.
    And smiled, for our intelligence.

'Now, Gentlemen of the Jury,' said
    The coroner – 'this woman's child
By misadventure met its death.'
    'Aye, aye,' said we. The mother smiled.

And I could see that child's one eye
    Which seemed to laugh, and say with glee:
'What caused my death you'll never know –
    Perhaps my mother murdered me.'

W. H. Davies

Low Barometer

The south-wind strengthens to a gale,
Across the moon the clouds fly fast,
The house is smitten as with a flail,
The chimney shudders to the blast.

On such a night, when Air has loosed
Its guardian grasp on blood and brain,
Old terrors then of god or ghost
Creep from their caves to life again;

And Reason kens he herits in
A haunted house. Tenants unknown
Assert their squalid lease of sin
With earlier title than his own.

Unbodied presences, the pack'd
Pollution and remorse of Time,
Slipp'd from oblivion reënact
The horrors of unhouseld crime.

Some men would quell the thing with prayer
Whose sightless footsteps pad the floor,
Whose fearful trespass mounts the stair
Or burts the lock'd forbidden door.

Some have seen corpses long interr'd
Escape from hallowing control,
Pale charnel forms—nay ev'n have heard
The shrilling of a troubled soul,

That wanders till the dawn hath cross'd
The dolorous dark, or Earth hath wound
Closer her storm-spredd cloke, and thrust
The baleful phantoms underground.

Robert Bridges

On a Return from Egypt

To stand here in the wings of Europe
disheartened, I have come away
from the sick land where in the sun lay
the gentle sloe-eyed murderers
of themselves, exquisites under a curse;
here to exercise my depleted fury.

For the heart is a coal, growing colder
when jewelled cerulean seas change
into grey rocks, grey water-fringe,
sea and sky altering like a cloth
till colour and sheen are gone both:
cold is an opiate of the soldier.

And all my endeavours are unlucky explorers
come back, abandoning the expedition;
the specimens, the lilies of ambition
still spring in their climate, still unpicked:
but time, time is all I lacked
to find them, as the great collectors before me.

The next month, then, there is a window
and with a crash I'll split the glass.
Behind it stands one I must kiss,
person of love or death
a person or a wraith,
I fear what I shall find.

Keith Douglas

The Souls of the Slain (extract)

I

The thick lids of Night closed upon me
Alone at the Bill
Of the Isle by the Race –
Many-caverned, bald, wrinkled of face –
And with darkness and silence the spirit was on me
To brood and be still.

II

No wind fanned the flats of the ocean,
Or promontory sides,
Or the ooze by the strand,
Or the bent-bearded slope of the land,
Whose base took its rest amid everlong motion
Of criss-crossing tides.

III

Soon from out of the Southward seemed nearing
A whirr, as of wings
Waved by mighty-vanned flies,
Or by night-moths of measureless size,
And in softness and smoothness well-nigh beyond hearing
Of corporal things.

IV

And they bore to the bluff, and alighted –
A dim-discerned train
Of sprites without mould,
Frameless souls none might touch or might hold –
On the ledge by the turreted lantern, far-sighted
By men of the main.

V

And I heard them say 'Home!' and I knew them
For souls of the felled
On the earth's nether bord
Under Capricorn, whither they'd warred,
And I neared in my awe, and gave heedfulness to them
With breathings inheld.

Thomas Hardy

Dead Men

To-night the moon inveigles them
to love: they infer from her gaze
her tacit encouragement.
To-night the white dresses and the jasmine scent
in the streets. I in another place
see the white dresses glimmer like moths. Come

to the west, out of that trance, my heart –
here the same hours have illumined
sleepers who are condemned or reprieved
and those whom their ambitions have deceived;
the dead men whom the wind
powders till they are like dolls: they to-night

rest in the sanitary earth perhaps
or where they died, no one has found them
or in their shallow graves the wild dog
discovered or exhumed a face or a leg
for food: the human virtue round them
is a vapour tasteless to a dog's chops.

All that is good of them, the dog consumes.
You would not know now the mind's flame is gone
more than the dog knows: you would forget
but that you see your own mind burning yet
and till you stifle in the ground will go on
burning the economical coal of your dreams.

Then leave the dead in the earth, an organism
not capable of resurrection, like mines,
less durable than the metal of a gun,
a casual meal for a dog, nothing but the bone
so soon. But to-night no lovers see the lines
of the moon's face as the lines of cynicism.

And the wise man is the lover
who in his planetary love revolves
without the traction of reason or time's control
and the wild dog finding meat in a hole
is a philosopher. The prudent mind resolves
on the lover's or the dog's attitude forever.

Keith Douglas

The Foreign Gate (extract)

The moon is a poor woman.
The moon returns to weep with us. The crosses
Burn raw and white upon the night's stiff banners.
The wooden crosses and the marble trees
Shrink from the foreign moon.
The iron gate glitters. Here the soldiers lie.
Fold up the flags, muffle the soldier's drum;
Silence the calling fife. O drape
The soldier's drum with heavy crêpe;
With mourning weeds muffle the soldier's girl.
It's a long way and a long march
To the returning moon and to the soil
No time at all.
O call
The soldier's glory by another name:
Shroud up the soldier's common shame
And drape the soldier's drum, but spare
The steel-caged brain, the feet that walk to war.

Once striding under a horsehair plume
Once beating the taut drums for war
The sunlight rang from brass and iron;
History was an angry play—
The boy grew tall and rode away;
The door hung slack; the pale girl wept
And cursed the company he kept.
And dumb men spoke
Through the glib mouths of smoke;
The servile learned to strike
The proud to shriek;
And strangled in their lovers' lips
The young fell short of glory in the sand
Raking for graves among the scattered sand;
The tattered flags strained at the wind
Scaring the thrifty kite, mocking the dead.
But muffle the soldier's drum, hide his pale head,
His face a spider's web of blood. O fold
The hands that grip a splintered gun.
The glittering gate
Baffles him still, his starvecrow soul. O drape
The soldier's drum and cry, who never dare
Defy the ironbound brain, the feet that walk to war.

Sidney Keyes

When You See Millions of the Mouthless Dead

When you see millions of the mouthless dead
Across your dreams in pale battalions go,
Say not soft things as other men have said,
That you'll remember. For you need not so.
Give them not praise. For, deaf, how should they know
It is not curses heaped on each gashed head?
Nor tears. Their blind eyes see not your tears flow.
Nor honour. It is easy to be dead.
Say only this, 'They are dead.' Then add thereto,
'Yet many a better one has died before.'
Then, scanning all the o'ercrowded mass, should you
Perceive one face that you loved heretofore,
It is a spook. None wears the face you knew.
Great death has made all his for evermore.

Charles Hamilton Sorley

The Unreturning

Suddenly night crushed out the day and hurled
Her remnants over cloud-peaks, thunder-walled.
Then fell a stillness such as harks appalled
When far-gone dead return upon the world.

There watched I for the Dead; but no ghost woke.
Each one whom Life exiled I named and called.
But they were all too far, or dumbed, or thralled;
And never one fared back to me or spoke.

Then peered the indefinite unshapen dawn
With vacant gloaming, sad as half-lit minds,
The weak-limned hour when sick men's sighs are drained.
And while I wondered on their being withdrawn,
Gagged by the smothering wing which none unbinds,
I dreaded even a heaven with doors so chained.

Wilfred Owen

Reconciliation

Word over all, beautiful as the sky,
Beautiful that war and all its deeds of carnage must in time be
    utterly lost;
That the hands of the sisters Death and Night incessantly softly
    wash again, and ever again, this soil'd world:
For my enemy is dead, a man divine as myself is dead,
I look where he lies white-faced and still in the coffin—I draw near;
Bend down and touch lightly with my lips the white face in the coffin.

Walt Whitman

Strange Meeting

It seemed that out of battle I escaped
Down some profound dull tunnel, long since scooped
Through granites which titanic wars had groined.

Yet also there encumbered sleepers groaned,
Too fast in thought or death to be bestirred.
Then, as I probed them, one sprang up, and stared
With piteous recognition in fixed eyes,
Lifting distressful hands, as if to bless.
And by his smile, I knew that sullen hall,—
By his dead smile I knew we stood in Hell.

With a thousand fears that vision's face was grained;
Yet no blood reached there from the upper ground,
And no guns thumped, or down the flues made moan.
"Strange friend," I said, "here is no cause to mourn."
"None," said that other, "save the undone years,
The hopelessness. Whatever hope is yours,
Was my life also; I went hunting wild
After the wildest beauty in the world,
Which lies not calm in eyes, or braided hair,
But mocks the steady running of the hour,
And if it grieves, grieves richlier than here.
For by my glee might many men have laughed,
And of my weeping something had been left,
Which must die now. I mean the truth untold,
The pity of war, the pity war distilled.
Now men will go content with what we spoiled,
Or, discontent, boil bloody, and be spilled.
They will be swift with swiftness of the tigress.
None will break ranks, though nations trek from progress.
Courage was mine, and I had mystery,
Wisdom was mine, and I had mastery:
To miss the march of this retreating world
Into vain citadels that are not walled.

Then, when much blood had clogged their chariot-wheels,
I would go up and wash them from sweet wells,
Even with truths that lie too deep for taint.
I would have poured my spirit without stint
But not through wounds; not on the cess of war.
Foreheads of men have bled where no wounds were.

"I am the enemy you killed, my friend.
I knew you in this dark: for so you frowned
Yesterday through me as you jabbed and killed.
I parried; but my hands were loath and cold.
Let us sleep now ..."

Wilfred Owen

Giving Back the Flower

So, because you chose to follow me into the subtle sadness of night,
And to stand in the half-set moon with the weird fall-light
on your glimmering hair,
Till your presence hid all of the earth and all of the sky from my sight,
And to give me a little scarlet bud, that was dying of frost, to wear,

Say, must you taunt me forever, forever? You looked at my hand and you knew
That I was the slave of the Ring, while you were as free as the wind is free.
When I saw your corpse in your coffin, I flung back your flower to you;
It was all of yours that I ever had; you must keep it, and—keep from me.

Ah? so God is your witness. Has God, then, no world to look after but ours?
May He not have been searching for that wild star, with the trailing plumage,
that flew
Far over a part of our darkness while we were there by the freezing flowers,
Or else brightening some planet's luminous rings, instead of thinking of you?

Or, if He was near us at all, do you think that He would sit listening there
Because you sang "Hear me, Norma," to a woman in jewels and lace,
While, so close to us, down in another street, in the wet, unlighted air,
There were children crying for bread and fire, and mothers who
questioned His grace?

Or perhaps He had gone to the ghastly field where the fight had been that day,
To number the bloody stabs that were there, to look at and judge the dead;
Or else to the place full of fever and moans where the wretched wounded lay;
At least I do not believe that He cares to remember a word that you said.

So take back your flower, I tell you—of its sweetness I now have no need;
Yes; take back your flower down into the stillness and mystery to keep;
When you wake I will take it, and God, then, perhaps will witness indeed,
But go, now, and tell Death he must watch you, and not let you
walk in your sleep.

Sarah Morgan Piatt

Windy Nights

Whenever the moon and stars are set,
Whenever the wind is high,
All night long in the dark and wet,
A man goes riding by.
Late in the night when the fires are out,
Why does he gallop and gallop about?

Whenever the trees are crying aloud,
And ships are tossed at sea,
By, on the highway, low and loud,
By at the gallop goes he.
By at the gallop he goes, and then
By he comes back at the gallop again.

Robert Louis Stevenson

The Ballad of Keith of Ravelston

The murmur of the mourning ghost
    That keeps the shadowy kine,
"O Keith of Ravelston,
    The sorrows of thy line!"

Ravelston, Ravelston,
    The merry path that leads
Down the golden morning hill,
    And thro' the silver meads;

Ravelston, Ravelston,
    The stile beneath the tree,
The maid that kept her mother's kine,
    The song that sang she!

She sang her song, she kept her kine,
    She sat beneath the thorn,
When Andrew Keith of Ravelston
    Rode thro' the Monday morn.

His henchman sing, his hawk-bells ring,
    His belted jewels shine;
O Keith of Ravelston,
    The sorrows of thy line!

Year after year, where Andrew came,
    Comes evening down the glade,
And still there sits a moonshine ghost
    Where sat the sunshine maid.

Her misty hair is faint and fair,
    She keeps the shadowy kine;
O Keith of Ravelston,
    The sorrows of thy line!

I lay my hand upon the stile,
    The stile is lone and cold,
The burnie that goes babbling by
    Says naught that can be told.

Yet, stranger! here, from year to year,
    She keeps her shadowy kine;
O Keith of Ravelston,
    The sorrows of thy line!

Step out three steps, where Andrew stood —
    Why blanch thy cheeks for fear?
The ancient stile is not alone,
    'Tis not the burn I hear!

She makes her immemorial moan,
    She keeps her shadowy kine;
O Keith of Ravelston,
    The sorrows of thy line!

Sydney Dobell

A Legend of Provence (extract)

The lights extinguished, by the hearth I leant,
Half weary with a listless discontent.
The flickering giant-shadows, gathering near,
Closed round me with a dim and silent fear.
All dull, all dark; save when the leaping flame,
Glancing, lit up a Picture's ancient frame.
Above the hearth it hung. Perhaps the night,
My foolish tremors, or the gleaming light,
Lent power to that Portrait dark and quaint –
A Portrait such as Rembrandt loved to paint –
The likeness of a Nun. I seemed to trace
A world of sorrow in the patient face,
In the thin hands folded across her breast –
Its own and the room's shadow hid the rest.
I gazed and dreamed, and the dull embers stirred,
Till an old legend that I once had heard
Came back to me; linked to the mystic gloom
Of that dark Picture in the ghostly room.

Adelaide Anne Procter

The Passing of Arthur (extract)

Then saw they how there hove a dusky barge,
Dark as a funeral scarf from stem to stern,
Beneath them; and descending they were ware
That all the decks were dense with stately forms;
Black-stoled, black-hooded, like a dream – by these
Three Queens with crowns of gold: and from them rose
A cry that shiver'd to the tingling stars,
And, as it were one voice, an agony
Of lamentation, like a wind that shrills
All night in a waste land where no one comes,
Or hath come since the making of the world.

Alfred, Lord Tennyson

The Shrouding of the Duchess of Malfi

Hark! Now everything is still,
The screech-owl and the whistler shrill,
Call upon our dame aloud,
And bid her quickly don her shroud!
Much you had of land and rent;
Your length in clay's now competent:
A long war disturbed your mind;
Here your perfect peace is signed.
Of what is't fools make such vain keeping?
Sin their conception, their birth weeping,
Their life a general mist of error,
Their death a hideous storm of terror.
Strew your hair with powders sweet,
Don clean linen, bathe your feet,
And—the foul fiend more to check—
A crucifix let bless your neck:
'Tis now full tide 'tween night and day;
End your groan and come away.

John Webster

Lady Alice

What doth the Lady Alice so late on the turret stair,
Without a lamp to light her, but the diamond in her hair;
When every arching passage overflows with shallow gloom,
And dreams float through the castle, into every silent room?

She trembles at her footsteps, although they fall so light;
For through the turret loopholes she sees the wild mid-night;
Broken vapours streaming across the stormy sky;
Down the empty corridors the blast doth moan and cry.

She steals along a gallery; she pauses by a door
And fast her tears are dropping down upon the oaken floor;
And thrice she seems returning – but thrice she turns again: –
Now heavy lie the cloud of sleep on that old father's brain!

Oh, well it were that *never* shouldst thou waken from thy sleep!
For wherefore should they waken, who waken but to weep?
No more, no more beside thy bed doth Peace a vigil keep,
But Woe, – a lion that awaits thy rousing for its leap.

An afternoon in April, no sun appears on high,
But a moist and yellow lustre fills the deepness of the sky:
And through the castle-gateway, left empty and forlorn,
Along the leafless avenue an honour'd bier is borne.

They stop. The long line closes up like some gigantic worm;
A shape is standing in the path, a wan and ghost-like form,
Which gazes fixedly; nor moves, nor utters any sound;
Then, like a statue built of snow, sinks down upon the ground.

And though her clothes are ragged, and though her feet are bare,
And though all wild and tangled falls her heavy silk-brown hair;
Though from her eyes the brightness, from her cheeks the bloom is fled,
They know their Lady Alice, the darling of the dead.

With silence, in her own old room the fainting form they lay,
Where all things stand unalter'd since the night she fled away:
But who – but who shall bring to life her father from the clay?
But who shall give her back again her heart of a former day?

William Allingham

Measure for Measure, Act III, Scene I (extract)

CLAUDIO: Death is a fearful thing.
ISABELLA: And shamèd life a hateful.
CLAUDIO: Ay, but to die, and go we know not where;
To lie in cold obstruction and to rot;
This sensible warm motion to become
A kneaded clod; and the delighted spirit
To bathe in fiery floods, or to reside
In thrilling region of thick-ribbèd ice;
To be imprisoned in the viewless winds,
And blown with restless violence round about
The pendent world; or to be worse than worst
Of those that lawless and incertain thought
Imagine howling! 'Tis too horrible!
The weariest and most loathèd worldly life
That age, ache, penury, and imprisonment
Can lay on nature is a paradise
To what we fear of death.

William Shakespeare

Elegy to the Memory of an Unfortunate Lady (extract)

What beckoning ghost, along the moonlight shade
Invites my step, and points to yonder glade?
'Tis she!—But why that bleeding bosom gored,
Why dimly gleams the visionary sword?

Alexander Pope

Triad

These be

Three silent things:

The falling snow . . *the hour*

Before the dawn . . the mouth of one

J U S T D E A D .

Adelaide Crapsey

L'Envoi

Where are the loves that we had loved before
When once we are alone, and shut the door?
No matter whose the arms that held me fast,
The arms of Darkness hold me at the last.
No matter down what primrose path I tend,
I kiss the lips of Silence in the end.
No matter on what heart I found delight,
I come again unto the breast of Night.
No matter when or how love did befall,
'Tis Loneliness that loves me best of all,
And in the end she claims me, and I know
That she will stay, though all the rest may go.
No matter whose the eyes that I would keep
Near in the dark, 'tis in the eyes of Sleep
That I must look and look forever more,
When once I am alone, and shut the door.

Willa Cather

The Phantom Wooer

A ghost, that loved a lady fair,
Ever in the starry air
Of midnight at her pillow stood;
And, with a sweetness skies above
The luring words of human love,
Her soul the phantom wooed.
Sweet and sweet is their poisoned note,
The little snakes of silver throat,
In mossy skulls that nest and lie,
Ever singing, "Die, oh! die."

Young soul, put off your flesh, and come
With me into the quiet tomb,
Our bed is lovely, dark, and sweet;
The earth will swing us, as she goes,
Beneath our coverlet of snows,
And the warm leaden sheet.
Dear and dear is their poisoned note,
The little snakes of silver throat,
In mossy skulls that nest and lie,
Ever singing, "Die, oh! Die."

Thomas Lovell Beddoes

The Ship of Death (extract)

I

Now it is autumn and the falling fruit
and the long journey towards oblivion.

The apples falling like great drops of dew
to bruise themselves an exit from themselves.

And it is time to go, to bid farewell
to one's own self, and find an exit
from the fallen self.

II

Have you built your ship of death, O have you?
O build your ship of death, for you will need it.

The grim frost is at hand, when the apples will fall
thick, almost thundrous, on the hardened earth.

And death is on the air like a smell of ashes!
Ah! can't you smell it?

And in the bruised body, the frightened soul
finds itself shrinking, wincing from the cold
that blows upon it through the orifices.

V

Build then the ship of death, for you must take
the longest journey, to oblivion.

And die the death, the long and painful death
that lies between the old self and the new.

Already our bodies are fallen, bruised, badly bruised,
already our souls are oozing through the exit
of the cruel bruise.

Already the dark and endless ocean of the end
is washing in through the breaches of our wounds,
already the flood is upon us.

Oh build your ship of death, your little ark
and furnish it with food, with little cakes, and wine
for the dark flight down oblivion.

VI

Piecemeal the body dies, and the timid soul
has her footing washed away, as the dark flood rises.

We are dying, we are dying, we are all of us dying
and nothing will stay the death-flood rising within us
and soon it will rise on the world, on the outside world.

We are dying, we are dying, piecemeal our bodies are dying
and our strength leaves us,
and our soul cowers naked in the dark rain over the flood,
cowering in the last branches of the tree of our life.

D. H. Lawrence

The Warnings

I was milking in the meadow when I heard the Banshee Keening:
Little birds were in the nest, lambs were on the lea,
Upon the brow o' the Fairy-hill a round gold moon was leaning—
She parted from the esker as the Banshee keened for me.

I was weaving by the door-post, when I heard the Death-watch beating:
And I signed the Cross upon me, and I spoke the Name of Three.
High and fair, through cloud and air, a silver moon was fleeting—
But the night began to darken as the Death-watch beat for me.

I was sleepless on my pillow when I heard the Dead man calling,
The Dead man that lies drowned at the bottom of the sea.
Down in the West, in wind and mist, a dim white moon was falling—
Now must I rise and go to him, the Dead who calls on me.

Alice Furlong

Come

Come, when the pale moon like a petal
    Floats in the pearly dusk of spring,
Come with outstretched arms to take me,
    Come with lips pursed up to cling.
Come, for life is a frail moth flying
    Caught in the web of the years that pass,
And soon we two, so warm and eager,
    Will be as the gray stones in the grass.

Sara Teasdale

Sung to the Condemned in Newgate Prison on the Eve of their Execution

All you that in the condemned hole do lie,
Prepare you, for tomorrow you shall die.
Watch all, and pray, the hour is drawing near,
That you before Almighty God will appear.
Examine well yourselves, in time repent,
That you not to eternal flames be sent,
And when St Sepulcher's bell tomorrow tolls,
The Lord above have mercy on your souls.

Anonymous

The Execution

On the night of the execution
a man at the door
mistook me for the coroner.
'Press,' I said.

But he didn't understand. He led me
into the wrong room
where the sheriff greeted me:
'You're late, Padre.'

'You're wrong,' I told him. 'I'm Press,'
'Yes, of course, Reverend Press.'
We went down a stairway.

'Ah, Mr Ellis,' said the Deputy.
'Press!' I shouted. But he shoved me
through a black curtain.
The lights were so bright
I couldn't see the faces
of the men sitting
opposite. But, thank God, I thought
they can see me!

'Look!' I cried. 'Look at my face!
Doesn't anybody know me?'

Then a hood covered my head.
'Don't make it harder for us,' the hangman whispered.

Alden Nowlan

Death

We are as maidens one and all,
In some shut convent place,
Pleased with the flowers, the service bells,
The cloister's shady grace,

That whiles, with fearful, fluttering hearts,
Look outward thro' the grate
And down the long white road, up which,
Some morning, soon or late,

Shall canter on his great grey horse
That splendid acred Lord
Who comes to lead us forth – his wife,
But half with our accord.

With fearful, fluttered hearts we wait –
We meet him, bathed in tears;
We are so loath to leave behind
Those tranquil convent years;

So loath to meet the pang, to take
(On some poor chance of bliss)
Life's labour on the windy sea
For a bower as still as this.

Weeping, we mount the crowded aisle,
And weeping after us
The bridesmaids follow – Come to me!
I will not meet you thus,

Pale rider to the convent gate.
Come, O rough bridegroom, Death,
Where, bashful bride, I wait you, veiled,
Flush-faced, with shaken breath;

I do not fear your kiss. I dream
New days, secure from strife,
And, bride-like, in the future hope –
A quiet household life.

Robert Louis Stevenson

Twilight Voices

Now, at the hour when ignorant mortals
Drowse in the shade of their whirling sphere,
Heaven and Hell from invisible portals
Breathing comfort and ghastly fear,
Voices I hear;
I hear strange voices, flitting, calling,
Wavering by on the dusky blast, –
"Come, let us go, for the night is falling;
Come, let us go, for the day is past!"

Troops of joys are they, now departed?
Wingèd hopes that no longer stay?
Guardian spirits grown weary-hearted?
Powers that have linger'd their latest day?
What do they say?
What do they sing? I hear them calling,
Whispering, gathering, flying fast, –
"Come, come, for the night is falling;
Come, come, for the day is past!"

Sing they to me? – "Thy taper's wasted;
Mortal, thy sands of life run low;
Thine hours like a flock of birds have hasted;
Time is ending; – we go! we go!"
Sing they so?
Mystical voices, floating, calling;
Dim farewells – the last, the last? –
"Come, come away, the night is falling;
Come, come away, the day is past!"

See, I am ready, Twilight Voices;
Child of the spirit-world am I;
How should I fear you? my soul rejoices.
O speak plainer! O draw nigh!
Fain would I fly!
Tell me your message, Ye who are calling
Out of the dimness vague and vast? –
Lift me, take me, – the night is falling;
Quick, let us go, – the day is past!

William Allingham

This Living Hand

This living hand, now warm and capable
Of earnest grasping, would, if it were cold
And in the icy silence of the tomb,
So haunt thy days and chill thy dreaming nights
That thou would wish thine own heart dry of blood
So in my veins red life might stream again,
And thou be conscience-calmed—see here it is—
I hold it towards you.

John Keats

Moon-Shadows

Still as
On windless nights
The moon-cast shadows are,
So still will be my heart when I
Am dead.

Adelaide Crapsey

At Last

O mother, open the window wide
    And let the daylight in;
The hills grow darker to my sight
    And thoughts begin to swim.

And mother dear, take my young son,
    (Since I was born of thee)
And care for all his little ways
    And nurse him on thy knee.

And mother, wash my pale pale hands
    And then bind up my feet;
My body may no longer rest
    Out of its winding sheet.

And mother dear, take a sapling twig
    And green grass newly mown,
And lay them on my empty bed
    That my sorrow be not known.

And mother, find three berries red
    And pluck them from the stalk,
And burn them at the first cockcrow
    That my spirit may not walk.

And mother dear, break a willow wand,
    And if the sap be even,
Then save it for sweet Robert's sake
    And he'll know my soul's in heaven.

And mother, when the big tears fall,
    (And fall, God knows, they may)
Tell him I died of my great love
    And my dying heart was gay.

And mother dear, when the sun has set
    And the pale kirk grass waves,
Then carry me through the dim twilight
    And hide me among the graves.

Elizabeth Siddal

All Hallows Night

Two things I did on Hallows Night:—
Made my house April-clear;
Left open wide my door
To the ghosts of the year.

Then one came in. Across the room
It stood up long and fair—
The ghost that was myself—
And gave me STARE for STARE.

Lizette Woodworth Reese

I Felt a Funeral, in My Brain

I felt a Funeral, in my Brain,
And Mourners to and fro
Kept treading - treading - till it seemed
That Sense was breaking through -

And when they all were seated,
A Service, like a Drum -
Kept beating - beating - till I thought
My mind was going numb -

And then I heard them lift a Box
And creak across my Soul
With those same Boots of Lead, again,
Then Space - began to toll,

As all the Heavens were a Bell,
And Being, but an Ear,
And I, and Silence, some strange Race,
Wrecked, solitary, here -

And then a Plank in Reason, broke,
And I dropped down, and down -
And hit a World, at every plunge,
And Finished knowing - then -

Emily Dickinson

The Lonely Death

In the cold I will rise, I will bathe
In waters of ice; myself
Will shiver, and shrive myself,
Alone in the dawn, and anoint
Forehead and feet and hands;
I will shutter the windows from light,
I will place in their sockets the four
Tall candles and set them aflame
In the grey of the dawn; and myself
Will lay myself straight in my bed,
And draw the sheet under my chin.

Adelaide Crapsey

The Ghosts

Pale shapes advancing from the mid-night air,
Beckoning with misty finger round my bed,
Bending your faded faces o'er my head,
I have no fear of ye! I seem to share
Your dim vitality – mine's well-nigh fled.
I feel the human outlines melt away;
These thin, gray hands that lie on the damp sheet
Are almost vapory enough to meet
Yours in the grasp of fellowship. My hair
Seems turning into cloud. The quickened clay
That walls me in is cracking, and I strive
Towards ye through the breach. Am I alive?
Or are ye dead? All's vague – a wide gray sea.
Hark! The cock crows! Now, spirits, welcome me!

Fitz-James O'Brien

Spring and Fall: To a Young Child

Márgarét, áre you gríeving
Over Goldengrove unleaving?
Leáves, líke the things of man, you
With your fresh thoughts care for, can you?
Áh! ás the heart grows older
It will come to such sights colder
By and by, nor spare a sigh
Though worlds of wanwood leafmeal lie;
And yet you *will* weep and know why.
Now no matter, child, the name:
Sórrow's spríngs áre the same.
Nor mouth had, no nor mind, expressed
What heart heard of, ghost guessed:
It ís the blight man was born for,
It is Margaret you mourn for.

Gerard Manley Hopkins

Fear

I am afraid, oh I am so afraid!
The cold black fear is clutching me to-night
As long ago when they would take the light
And leave the little child who would have prayed,
Frozen and sleepless at the thought of death.
My heart that beats too fast will rest too soon;
I shall not know if it be night or noon, —
Yet shall I struggle in the dark for breath?
Will no one fight the Terror for my sake,
The heavy darkness that no dawn will break?
How can they leave me in that dark alone,
Who loved the joy of light and warmth so much,
And thrilled so with the sense of sound and touch, —
How can they shut me underneath a stone?

Sara Teasdale

Flash

I am less of myself and more of the sun;
The beat of life is wearing me
To an incomplete oblivion,
Yet not to the certain dignity
Of death. *They cannot even die*
Who have not lived.

The hungry jaws
Of space snap at my unlearned eye,
And time tears in my flesh like claws.

If I am not life's, if I am not death's,
Out of chaos I must re-reap
The burden of untasted breaths.
Who has not waked may not yet sleep.

Hazel Hall

Sonnet 26 (extract from Later Life)

This Life is full of numbness and of balk,
Of haltingness and baffled short-coming,
Of promise unfulfilled, of everything
That is puffed vanity and empty talk:
Its very bud hangs cankered on the stalk,
Its very song-bird trails a broken wing,
Its very Spring is not indeed like Spring,
But sighs like Autumn round an aimless walk.
This Life we live is dead for all its breath;
Death's self it is, set off on pilgrimage,
Travelling with tottering steps the first short stage:
The second stage is one mere desert dust
Where Death sits veiled amid creation's rust: –
Unveil thy face, O Death who art not Death.

Christina Rossetti

The Dream

I dreamed that, buried in my fellow clay,
Close by a common beggar's side I lay;
And as so mean a neighbour shocked my pride,
Thus, like a corpse of consequence, I cried:
'Scoundrel, begone, and henceforth touch me not;
More manners learn, and at a distance rot.'
'How, scoundrel!' in a haughtier tone cried he:
'Proud lump of dirt, I scorn thy words and thee.
Here all are equal, now thy case is mine:
This is my rotting-place, and that is thine.'

Anonymous

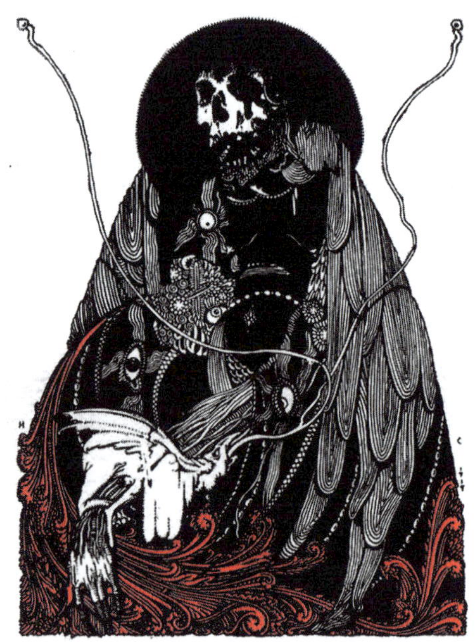

The Sick Rose

O Rose, thou art sick!
The invisible worm
That flies in the night,
In the howling storm,
Has found out thy bed
Of crimson joy,
And his dark secret love
Does thy life destroy.

William Blake

The Hurry of the Spirits, in a Fever and Nervous Disorders (extract)

Who can describe them? Fragments of old dreams,
Borrowed from midnight, torn from fairy fields
And fairy skies, and regions of the dead,
Abrupt, ill-sorted. O 'tis all confusion!
If I but close my eyes, strange images
In thousand forms and thousand colours rise,
Stars, rainbows, moons, green dragons, bears, and ghosts,
An endless medley, rush upon the stage,
And dance and riot wild in reason's court
Above control. I'm in a raging storm,
Where seas and skies are blended, while my soul
Like some light worthless chip of floating cork
Is tossed from wave to wave: now overwhelmed
With breaking floods I drown, and seem to lose
All being; now high-mounted on the ridge
Of a tall foaming surge, I'm all at once
Caught up into the storm, and ride the wind,
The whistling wind; unmanageable steed,
And feeble rider!

Isaac Watts

Lines Written During a Period of Insanity

Hatred and vengeance, my eternal portion,
Scarce can endure delay of execution,
Wait, with impatient readiness, to seize my
Soul in a moment.

Damned below Judas: more abhorred than he was,
Who for a few pence sold his holy Master.
Twice betrayed Jesus me, the last delinquent,
Deems the profanest.

Man disavows, and Deity disowns me:
Hell might afford my miseries a shelter;
Therefore hell keeps her ever-hungry mouths all
Bolted against me.

Hard lot! encompassed with a thousand dangers;
Weary, faint, trembling with a thousand terrors,
I'm called, if vanquished, to receive a sentence
Worse than Abiram's.

Him the vindictive rod of angry justice
Sent quick and howling to the center headlong;
I, fed with judgment, in a fleshly tomb, am
Buried above ground.

William Cowper

On a Frightful Dream

This morn, ere yet had rung the matin peal,
    The cursèd Merlin with his potent spell
    Aggrieved me sore, and from his wizard cell
    (First fixing on mine eyes a magic seal)
Millions of ghosts and shadowy shapes let steal,
    Who, swarming round my couch, with horrid yell
    Chattered and mowed, as though from deepest hell
    They had escaped.—I oft, with fervent zeal
Essayed, and prayer, to mar th' Enchanter's pow'r.
    In vain; for thicker still the crew came on,
    And now had weighed me down, but that the day
Appeared, and Phoebus, from his eastern tow'r,
    With new-tricked beam like Truth immortal shone,
    And chased the visionary forms away.

John Codrington Bampfylde

On The Wing

Once in a dream (for once I dreamed of you)
    We stood together in an open field;
    Above our heads two swift-winged pigeons wheeled,
Sporting at east and courting full in view.
When loftier still a broadening darkness flew,
    Down-swooping, and a ravenous hawk revealed;
    Too weak to fight, too fond to fly, they yield;
So farewell life and love and pleasures new.
Then as their plumes fell fluttering to the ground,
    Their snow-white plumage flecked with crimson drops,
        I wept, and thought I turned towards you to weep:
    But you were gone; while rustling hedgerow tops
Bent in a wind which bore to me a sound
        Of far-off piteous bleat of lambs and sheep.

Christina Rossetti

Images

Her skirt lifted as a dark mist
From the columns of amethyst.

The lark crawls on the cloud
Like a flea on a white body.

The after-black lies low along the hills
Like the trailed smoke of a steamer.

T. E. Hulme

Secrets

Secrets
infesting my half-sleep ...
did you enter my wound from another wound
brushing mine in a crowd ...
or did I snare you on my sharper edges
as a bird flying through cobwebbed trees at sun-up
carries off spiders on its wings?

Secrets,
running over my soul without sound,
only when dawn comes tip-toeing
ushered by a suave wind,
and dreams disintegrate
like breath shapes in frosty air,
I shall overhear you, bare-foot,
scatting off into the darkness ...
I shall know you, secrets
by the litter you have left
and by your bloody foot-prints.

Lola Ridge

Dejection: An Ode (extract)

Hence, viper thoughts, that coil around my mind,
    Reality's dark dream!
I turn from you, and listen to the wind,
    Which long has raved unnoticed. What a scream
Of agony by torture lengthened out
That lute sent forth! Thou Wind, that rav'st without,
    Bare crag, or mountain tairn, or blasted tree,
Or pine-grove whither woodman never clomb,
Or lonely house, long held—the witches' home,
    Methinks were fitter instruments for thee,
Mad lutanist! who in this month of showers,
Of dark-brown gardens, and of peeping flowers,
Mak'st devils' yule, with worse than wintry song,
The blossoms, buds, and timorous leaves among.
    Thou actor, perfect in all tragic sounds!

Samuel Taylor Coleridge

Samson Agonistes (extract)

Then had I not been thus exiled from light,
As in the land of darkness yet in light,
To live a life half dead, a living death,
And buried; but O yet more miserable!
Myself my sepulchre, a moving grave,
Buried, yet not exempt
By privilege of death and burial
From worst of other evils, pains, and wrongs,
But made hereby obnoxious more
To all the miseries of life,
Life in captivity
Among inhuman foes.

John Milton

Ode on Melancholy

No, no, go not to Lethe, neither twist
    Wolf's-bane, tight-rooted, for its poisonous wine;
Nor suffer thy pale forehead to be kiss'd
    By nightshade, ruby grape of Proserpine;
Make not your rosary of yew-berries,
    Nor let the beetle, nor the death-moth be
        Your mournful Psyche, nor the downy owl
A partner in your sorrow's mysteries;
    For shade to shade will come too drowsily,
        And drown the wakeful anguish of the soul.

But when the melancholy fit shall fall
    Sudden from heaven like a weeping cloud,
That fosters the droop-headed flowers all,
    And hides the green hill in an April shroud;
Then glut thy sorrow on a morning rose,
    Or on the rainbow of the salt sand-wave,
        Or on the wealth of globed peonies;
Or if thy mistress some rich anger shows,
    Emprison her soft hand, and let her rave,
        And feed deep, deep upon her peerless eyes.

She dwells with Beauty – Beauty that must die;
    And Joy, whose hand is ever at his lips
Bidding adieu; and aching Pleasure nigh,
    Turning to poison while the bee-mouth sips:
Ay, in the very temple of Delight
    Veil'd Melancholy has her sovran shrine,
        Though seen of none save him whose strenuous tongue
    Can burst Joy's grape against his palate fine;
His soul shalt taste the sadness of her might,
        And be among her cloudy trophies hung.

John Keats

Felo de Se

With Apologies to Mr Swinburne

For repose I have sighed and have struggled; have sigh'd and have struggled in vain
I am held in the Circle of Being and caught in the Circle of Pain.
I was wan and weary with life; my sick soul yearned for death;
I was weary of women and war and the sea and the wind's wild breath;
I cull'd sweet poppies and crush'd them, the blood ran rich and red: –
And I cast it in crystal chalice and drank of it till I was dead.
And the mould of the man was mute, pulseless in ev'ry part,
The long limbs lay on the sand with an eagle eating the heart.
Repose for the rotting head and peace for the putrid breast,
But for that which is 'I' indeed the gods have decreed no rest;
No rest but an endless aching, a sorrow which grows amain: –
I am caught in the Circle of Being and held in the Circle of Pain.
Bitter indeed is Life, and bitter of Life the breath,
But give me Life and its ways and its men, if this be Death.
Wearied I once of the Sun and the voices which clamour'd around:
Give them me back – in the sightless depths there is neither light nor sound.
Sick is my soul, and sad and feeble and faint as it felt
When (far, dim day) in the fair flesh-fane of the body it dwelt.
But then I could run to the shore, weeping and weary and weak;
See the waves' blue sheen and feel the breath of the breeze on my cheek:
Could wail with the wailing wind; strike sharply the hands in despair;
Could shriek with the shrieking blast, grow frenzied and tear the hair;
Could fight fierce fights with the foe or clutch at a human hand;
And weary could lie at length on the soft, sweet, saffron sand ...
I have neither a voice nor hands, nor any friend nor a foe;
I am I – just a Pulse of Pain – I am I, that is all I know.
For Life, and the sickness of Life, and Death and desire to die; –
They have passed away like the smoke, here is nothing but Pain and I.

Amy Levy

Invictus

Out of the night that covers me,
Black as the Pit from pole to pole,
I thank whatever gods may be
For my unconquerable soul.

In the fell clutch of circumstance
I have not winced nor cried aloud.
Under the bludgeonings of chance
My head is bloody, but unbowed.

Beyond this place of wrath and tears
Looms but the Horror of the shade,
And yet the menace of the years
Finds, and shall find, me unafraid.

It matters not how strait the gate,
How charged with punishments the scroll,
I am the master of my fate;
I am the captain of my soul.

William Ernest Henley

SILENCE

Chapter Three

Dark Landscapes

"Now is hell landed here upon the earth"

'Lucifer Ascending', Thomas Middleton

Alone

From childhood's hour I have not been
As others were—I have not seen
As others saw—I could not bring
My passions from a common spring—
From the same source I have not taken
My sorrow—I could not awaken
My heart to joy at the same tone—
And all I lov'd—*I* lov'd alone—
Then—in my childhood—in the dawn
Of a most stormy life—was drawn
From ev'ry depth of good and ill
The mystery which binds me still—
From the torrent, or the fountain—
From the red cliff of the mountain—
From the sun that 'round me roll'd
In its autumn tint of gold—
From the lightning in the sky
As it pass'd me flying by—
From the thunder, and the storm—
And the cloud that took the form
(When the rest of Heaven was blue)
Of a demon in my view—

Edgar Allan Poe

A Tragedy

Who's that walking on the moorland?
Who's that moving on the hill?
They are passing 'mid the bracken,
But the shadows grow and blacken
And I cannot see them clearly on the hill.

Who's that calling on the moorland?
Who's that crying on the hill?
Was it bird or was it human,
Was it child, or man, or woman,
Who was calling so sadly on the hill?

Who's that running on the moorland?
Who's that flying on the hill?
He is there – and there again,
But you cannot see him plain,
For the shadow lies so darkly on the hill.

What's that lying in the heather?
What's that lurking on the hill?
My horse will go no nearer,
And I cannot see it clearer,
But there's something that is lying on the hill.

Arthur Conan Doyle

Across the Red Sky

Across the red sky two birds flying
Flying with drooping wings
Silent and solitary their ominous flight.
All day the triumphant sun with yellow banners
Warred and warred with the earth, and when she yieldéd
Stabbed her heart, gathered her blood in a chalice
Spilling it over the evening sky.
When the dark plumaged birds go flying flying
Quiet lies the earth wrapt in her mournful shadow
Her sightless eyes turned to the red sky
And the restlessly seeking birds.

Katherine Mansfield

November Night

Listen ...
With faint dry sound,
Like steps of passing ghosts,
The leaves, frost-crisped, break from the trees
And fall.

Adelaide Crapsey

Turn Not Now for Comfort Here

Turn not now for comfort here;
    The lamps are quenched, the moors are gone;
Cold and lonely, dim and drear,
    Void are now those hills of stone.

Sadly sighing, Anvale woods
    Whisper peace to my decay;
Fir-tree over pine-tree broods
    Dark and high and piled away.

Gone are all who saw my glory
    Fill on festal nights the trees
Distant lit, now silver hoary,
    Bowed they to the freshening breeze.

They are dead who heard at night
    Woods and winds and waters sound,
Where my casements cast their light
    Red upon the snow-piled ground.

Some from afar in foreign regions,
    Some from drear suffering – wild unrest,
All light on land and winged legions
    Fill the old woods and parent nest.

Charlotte Brontë

The Villain

While joy gave clouds the light of stars,
That beamed where'er they looked;
And calves and lambs had tottering knees,
Excited, while they sucked;
While every bird enjoyed his song,
Without one thought of harm or wrong –
I turned my head and saw the wind,
Not far from where I stood,
Dragging the corn by her golden hair,
Into a dark and lonely wood.

W. H. Davies

The Crazed Moon

Crazed through much child-bearing
The moon is staggering in the sky;
Moon-struck by the despairing
Glances of her wandering eye
We grope, and grope in vain,
For children born of her pain.

Children dazed or dead!
When she in all her virginal pride
First trod on the mountain's head
What stir ran through the countryside
Where every foot obeyed her glance!
What manhood led the dance!

Fly-catchers of the moon,
Our hands are blenched, our fingers seem
But slender needles of bone;
Blenched by that malicious dream
They are spread wide that each
May rend what comes in reach.

W. B. Yeats

Why Do I Hate That Lone Green Dell

Why do I hate that lone green dell?
Buried in moors and mountains wild
That is a spot I had loved too well
Had I but seen it when a child.

There are bones whitening there in the summer's heat,
But it is not for that, and none can tell;
None but one can the secret repeat
Why I hate that lone green dell.

Noble foe, I pardon thee
All thy cold and scornful pride,
For thou wast a priceless friend to me
When my sad heart had none beside.

And, leaning on thy generous arm
A breath of old times over me came;
The earth shone round with a long-lost charm;
Alas, I forgot I was not the same.

Before a day – an hour – passed by
My spirit knew itself once more;
I saw the gilded vapours fly
And leave me as I was before.

Emily Brontë

The Cold Earth Slept Below

The cold earth slept below;
Above the cold sky shone;
And all around,
With a chilling sound,
From caves of ice and fields of snow
The breath of night like death did flow
Beneath the sinking moon.

The wintry hedge was black;
The green grass was not seen;
The birds did rest
On the bare thorn's breast,
Whose roots, beside the pathway track,
Had bound their folds o'er many a crack
Which the frost had made between.

Thine eyes glow'd in the glare
Of the moon's dying light;
As a fen-fire's beam
On a sluggish stream
Gleams dimly—so the moon shone there,
And it yellow'd the strings of thy tangled hair,
That shook in the wind of night.

The moon made thy lips pale, beloved;
The wind made thy bosom chill;
The night did shed
On thy dear head
Its frozen dew, and thou didst lie
Where the bitter breath of the naked sky
Might visit thee at will.

Percy Bysshe Shelley

Prophecy

I shall die hidden in a hut
    In the middle of an alder wood,
With the back door blind and bolted shut,
    And the front door locked for good.

I shall lie folded like a saint,
    Lapped in a scented linen sheet,
On a bedstead striped with bright-blue paint,
    Narrow and cold and neat.

The midnight will be glassy black
    Behind the panes, with wind about
To set his mouth against a crack
    And blow the candle out.

Elinor Wylie

Wilderspin

In the little red house by the river,
    When the short night fell,
Beside his web sat the weaver,
    Weaving a twisted spell.
Mary and the Saints deliver
    My soul from the nethermost Hell!

In the little red house by the rushes
    It grew not dark at all,
For day dawned over the bushes
    Before the night could fall.
Where now a torrent rushes,
    The brook ran thin and small.

In the little red house a chamber
    Was set with jewels fair;
There did a vine clamber
    Along the clambering stair,
And grapes that shone like amber
    Hung at the windows there.

Will the loom not cease whirring?
    Will the house never be still?
Is never a horseman stirring
    Out and about on the hill?
Was it the cat purring?
    Did some one knock at the sill?

To the little red house a rider
    Was bound to come that night.
A cup of sheeny cider
    Stood ready for his delight.
And like a great black spider,
    The weaver watched on the right.

To the little red house by the river
    I came when the short night fell.
I broke the web for ever,
    I broke my heart as well.
Michael and the Saints deliver
    My soul from the nethermost Hell!

Mary Coleridge

Captivity

Caged in old woods, whose reverend echoes wake
When the hern screams along the distant lake,
Her little heart oft flutters to be free,
Oft sighs to turn THE UNRELENTING KEY.
IN VAIN! the nurse that rusted relic wears,
Nor mov'd by gold – nor to be mov'd by tears;
And terraced walls their black reflection throw
On the green-mantled moat that SLEEPS BELOW.

Samuel Rogers

Mariana (extract)

With blackest moss the flower-plots
    Were thickly crusted, one and all:
The rusted nails fell from the knots
    That held the pear to the gable-wall.
The broken sheds looked sad and strange:
    Unlifted was the clinking latch;
    Weeded and worn the ancient thatch
Upon the lonely moated grange.
        She only said, "My life is dreary,
          He cometh not," she said;
        She said, "I am aweary, aweary,
        I would that I were dead!"

All day within the dreamy house,
    The doors upon their hinges creaked;
The blue fly sung in the pane; the mouse
    Behind the moldering wainscot shrieked,
Or from the crevice peered about.
    Old faces glimmered through the doors,
    Old footsteps trod the upper floors,
Old voices called her from without.
        She only said, "My life is dreary,
          He cometh not," she said;
        She said, "I am aweary, aweary,
        I would that I were dead!"

The sparrow's chirrup on the roof,
    The slow clock ticking, and the sound
Which to the wooing wind aloof
    The poplar made, did all confound
Her sense; but most she loathed the hour
    When the thick-moted sunbeam lay
    Athwart the chambers, and the day
Was sloping toward his western bower.
        Then said she, "I am very dreary,
          He will not come," she said;
        She wept, "I am aweary, aweary,
        Oh God, that I were dead!"

Alfred, Lord Tennyson

Bluebeard's Closet

Fasten the chamber!
Hide the red key;
Cover the portal,
That eyes may not see.
Get thee to market,
To wedding and prayer;
Labor or revel,
The chamber is there!

In comes a stranger –
"Thy pictures how fine,
Titian or Guido,
Whose is the sign?"
Looks he behind them?
Ah! have a care!
"Here is a finer."
The chamber is there!

Fair spreads the banquet,
Rich the array;
See the bright torches
Mimicking day;
When harp and viol
Thrill the soft air,
Comes a light whisper:
The chamber is there!

Marble and painting,
Jasper and gold,
Purple from Tyrus,
Fold upon fold,
Blossoms and jewels,
Thy palace prepare:
Pale grows the monarch;
The chamber is there!

Once it was open
As shore to the sea;
White were the turrets,
Goodly to see;
All through the casements
Flowed the sweet air;
Now it is darkness;
The chamber is there!

Silence and horror
Brood on the walls;
Through every crevice
A little voice calls:
"Quicken, mad footsteps,
On pavement and stair;
Look not behind thee,
The chamber is there!

Out of the gateway,
Through the wide world,
Into the tempest
Beaten and hurled,
Vain is thy wandering,
Sure thy despair,
Flying or staying,
The chamber is there!

Rose Terry Cooke

The Haunted Palace

In the greenest of our valleys
By good angels tenanted,
Once a fair and stately palace—
Radiant palace—reared its head.
In the monarch Thought's dominion,
It stood there!
Never seraph spread a pinion
Over fabric half so fair!

Banners yellow, glorious, golden,
On its roof did float and flow,
(This—all this—was in the olden
Time long ago)
And every gentle air that dallied,
In that sweet day,
Along the ramparts plumed and pallid,
A wingèd odor went away.

Wanderers in that happy valley,
Through two luminous windows, saw
Spirits moving musically,
To a lute's well-tunèd law,
Round about a throne where, sitting
Porphyrogene!
In state his glory well befitting,
The ruler of the realm was seen.

And all with pearl and ruby glowing
Was the fair palace door,
Through which came flowing, flowing, flowing
And sparkling evermore,
A troop of Echoes, whose sweet duty
Was but to sing,
In voices of surpassing beauty,
The wit and wisdom of their king.

But evil things, in robes of sorrow,
Assailed the monarch's high estate;
(Ah, let us mourn!—for never morrow
Shall dawn upon him, desolate!)
And round about his home the glory
That blushed and bloomed
Is but a dim-remembered story
Of the old time entombed.

And travellers now, within that valley,
Through the red-litten windows see
Vast forms that move fantastically
To a discordant melody;
While, like a ghastly rapid river,
Through the pale door
A hideous throng rush out forever
And laugh—but smile no more.

Edgar Allan Poe

The New House

Now first, as I shut the door,
I was alone
In the new house; and the wind
Began to moan.

Old at once was the house,
And I was old;
My ears were teased with the dread
Of what was foretold,

Nights of storm, days of mist, without end;
Sad days when the sun
Shone in vain: old griefs and griefs
Not yet begun.

All was foretold me; naught
Could I foresee;
But I learned how the wind would sound
After these things should be.

Edward Thomas

The Gray Folk

The house, with blind unhappy face,
    Stands lonely in the last year's corn,
    And in the grayness of the morn
The gray folk come about the place.

By many pathways, gliding gray
    They come past meadow, wood, and wold,
    Come by the farm and by the fold
From the green fields of yesterday.

Past lock and chain and bolt and bar
    They press, to stand about my bed,
    And like the faces of the dead
I know their hidden faces are.

They will not leave me in the day
    And when night falls they will not go,
    Because I silenced, long ago,
The only voice that they obey.

Edith Nesbit

The Haunted House (extract)

O, very gloomy is the house of woe,
Where tears are falling while the bell is knelling,
With all the dark solemnities that show
That Death is in the dwelling!

O, very, very dreary is the room
Where Love, domestic Love, no longer nestles,
But smitten by the common stroke of doom,
The corpse lies on the trestles!

But house of woe, and hearse, and sable pall,
The narrow home of the departed mortal,
Ne'er looked so gloomy as that Ghostly Hall,
With its deserted portal!

The centipede along the threshold crept,
The cobweb hung across in mazy tangle,
And in its winding sheet the maggot slept,
At every nook and angle.

The very stains and fractures on the wall,
Assuming features solemn and terrific,
Hinted some tragedy of that old hall,
Locked up in hieroglyphic.

Some tale that might, perchance, have solved the doubt,
Wherefore, among those flags so dull and livid;
The banner of the bloody hand shone out
So ominously vivid.

For over all there hung a cloud of fear,
A sense of mystery the spirit daunted,
And said, as plain as whisper in the ear,
The place is haunted!

Prophetic hints that filled the soul with dread,
But through one gloomy entrance pointing mostly,
The while some secret inspiration said,
"That chamber is the ghostly!"

Across the door no gossamer festoon
Swung pendulous, – no web, no dusty fringes,
No silky chrysalis or white cocoon,
About its nooks and hinges.

The spider shunned the interdicted room,
The moth, the beetle, and the fly were banished,
And when the sunbeam fell athwart the gloom,
The very midge had vanished.

One lonely ray that glanced upon a bed,
As if with awful aim direct and certain,
To show the Bloody Hand in burning red,
Embroidered on the curtain.

Thomas Hood

The Sleeper

At midnight, in the month of June,
I stand beneath the mystic moon.
An opiate vapor, dewy, dim,
Exhales from out her golden rim,
And softly dripping, drop by drop,
Upon the quiet mountain top,
Steals drowsily and musically
Into the universal valley.
The rosemary nods upon the grave;
The lily lolls upon the wave;
Wrapping the fog about its breast,
The ruin moulders into rest;
Looking like Lethe, see! the lake
A conscious slumber seems to take,
And would not, for the world, awake.
All Beauty sleeps!—and lo! where lies
Irene, with her Destinies!

Oh, lady bright! can it be right—
This window open to the night?
The wanton airs, from the tree-top,
Laughingly through the lattice drop—
The bodiless airs, a wizard rout,
Flit through thy chamber in and out,
And wave the curtain canopy
So fitfully—so fearfully—
Above the closed and fringéd lid
'Neath which thy slumb'ring soul lies hid,
That, o'er the floor and down the wall,
Like ghosts the shadows rise and fall!
Oh, lady dear, hast thou no fear?
Why and what art thou dreaming here?
Sure thou art come o'er far-off seas,
A wonder to these garden trees!
Strange is thy pallor! strange thy dress!
Strange, above all, thy length of tress,
And this all solemn silentness!

The lady sleeps! Oh, may her sleep,
Which is enduring, so be deep!
Heaven have her in its sacred keep!
This chamber changed for one more holy,
This bed for one more melancholy,
I pray to God that she may lie
Forever with unopened eye,
While the pale sheeted ghosts go by!

My love, she sleeps! Oh, may her sleep,
As it is lasting, so be deep!
Soft may the worms about her creep!
Far in the forest, dim and old,
For her may some tall vault unfold—
Some vault that oft hath flung its black
And wingéd pannels fluttering back,
Triumphant, o'er the crested palls
Of her grand family funerals—

Some sepulchre, remote, alone,
Against whose portals she hath thrown,
In childhood, many an idle stone—
Some tomb from out whose sounding door
She ne'er shall force an echo more,
Thrilling to think, poor child of sin!
It was the dead who groaned within.

Edgar Allan Poe

Haunted Houses

All houses wherein men have lived and died
Are haunted houses. Through the open doors
The harmless phantoms on their errands glide,
With feet that make no sound upon the floors.

We meet them at the door-way, on the stair,
Along the passages they come and go,
Impalpable impressions on the air,
A sense of something moving to and fro.

There are more guests at table than the hosts
Invited; the illuminated hall
Is thronged with quiet, inoffensive ghosts,
As silent as the pictures on the wall.

The stranger at my fireside cannot see
The forms I see, nor hear the sounds I hear;
He but perceives what is; while unto me
All that has been is visible and clear.

We have no title-deeds to house or lands;
Owners and occupants of earlier dates
From graves forgotten stretch their dusty hands,
And hold in mortmain still their old estates.

The spirit-world around this world of sense
Floats like an atmosphere, and everywhere
Wafts through these earthly mists and vapours dense
A vital breath of more ethereal air.

Our little lives are kept in equipoise
By opposite attractions and desires;
The struggle of the instinct that enjoys,
And the more noble instinct that aspires.

These perturbations, this perpetual jar
Of earthly wants and aspirations high,
Come from the influence of an unseen star
An undiscovered planet in our sky.

And as the moon from some dark gate of cloud
Throws o'er the sea a floating bridge of light,
Across whose trembling planks our fancies crowd
Into the realm of mystery and night,—

So from the world of spirits there descends
A bridge of light, connecting it with this,
O'er whose unsteady floor, that sways and bends,
Wander our thoughts above the dark abyss.

Henry Wadsworth Longfellow

Introspection

That house across the road is full of ghosts.
The windows, all inquisitive, look inward.
All are shut.
I've never seen a body in the house.
Have you? Have you?
Yet feet go sounding in the corridors,
And up and down, and up and down the stairs,
All day, all night, all day.

When will the show begin?
When will the host be in?
What is the preparation for?
When will he open the bolted door?
When will the minutes move smoothly along in their hours?
Time, answer!

(Can you see a feverish face
Pressing at the window-pane?)

The air must be hot: how hot inside.
If only somebody could go
And snap the windows open wide,
And keep them so!

All the back rooms are very large, and there
(So it is said)
They sit before their open books and stare.
Or one will rise and sadly shake his head,
Another will comb out her languid hair;
While some will move untiringly about
Through all the rooms, for ever in and out,
Or up and down the stair;

Or gaze into the desolate back-garden
And talk about the rain,
Then drift back from the window to the table,
Folding long hands, to sit and think again.

They can never meet like homely people
Round a fireside
After daily work ...
Always busy with procrastination,
Backward and forward they move in the house,
Full of their questions
No one can answer.
Nothing will happen ... Nothing will happen ...

Harold Monro

The Lady of the Manor (extract)

Next died the Lady who yon Hall possessed;
And here they brought her noble bones to rest.
In Town she dwelt;—forsaken stood the Hall:
Worms ate the floors, the tapestry fled the wall:
No fire the kitchen's cheerless grate displayed;
No cheerful light the long-closed sash conveyed;
The crawling worm, that turns a summer-fly,
Here spun his shroud and laid him up to die
The winter-death:—upon the bed of state,
The bat shrill-shrieking wooed his flickering mate;
To empty rooms the curious came no more,
From empty cellars turned the angry poor,
And surly beggars cursed the ever-bolted door.

George Crabbe

In Memoriam A. H. H. (extract)

II

Old Yew, which graspest at the stones
  That name the under-lying dead,
  Thy fibers net the dreamless head,
Thy roots are wrapt about the bones.

The seasons bring the flower again,
  And bring the firstling to the flock;
  And in the dusk of thee, the clock
Beats out the little lives of men.

O not for thee the glow, the bloom,
  Who changest not in any gale,
  Nor branding summer suns avail
To touch thy thousand years of gloom:

And gazing on thee, sullen tree,
  Sick for thy stubborn hardihood,
  I seem to fail from out my blood
And grow incorporate into thee.

Alfred, Lord Tennyson

The Haunted Wood (extract)

I ofttimes come to this lonely place,
And forget the stir of my restless race;
Forget the woes of human life,
The bitter pang and the constant strife,
The angry word and the cruel taunt,
The sight and the sound of guilt and want,
And the frequent tear by the widow shed,
When her infants ask in vain for bread.
All these I put from my mind aside,
And forget the offence of worldly pride.

It is said that the Spirits of buried men
Oft come to this wicked world again;
That the churchyard turf is often trod
By the unlaid tenants of tomb and sod,
That the midnight sea itself is swept,
By those who have long beneath it slept.
And they say of this old, mossy wood,
Whose hoary trunks have for ages stood,
That every knoll and dim-lit glade
Is haunted at night by its restless Shade.

Isaac McLellan

The Progress of Poetry

I saw a Gardener with a watering can
Sprinkling dejectedly the heads of men
Buried up to their necks in the wet clay.

I saw a Bishop born in sober black
With a bewildered look on his small face
Being rocked in a cradle by a grey-haired woman.

I saw a man, with an air of painful duty,
Binding his privates up with bunches of ribbon.
The woman who helped him was decently veiled in white.

I said to the Gardener: 'When I was a younger poet
At least my reference to death had some sonority.
I sang the danger and the deeps of love.

Is the world poxy with a fresh disease?
Or is this a maggot I feel here, gnawing my breast
And wrinkling my five senses like a walnut's kernel?'

The Gardener answered: 'I am more vexed by the lichen
Upon my walls. I scraped it off with a spade.
As I did so I heard a very human scream.

'In evening's sacred cool, among my bushes
A Figure was wont to walk. I deemed it angel.
But look at the footprint. There's hair between the toes!'

Christopher Caudwell

The Grave

Whilst some affect the sun, and some the shade,
Some flee the city, some the hermitage,
Their aims as various as the roads they take
In journeying through life—the task be mine,
To paint the gloomy horrors of the tomb,
Th' appointed place of rendezvous, where all
These travellers meet. Thy succours I implore,
Eternal King! whose potent arm sustains
The keys of hell and death. The Grave, dread thing!
Men shiver when thou'rt named: Nature, appalled
Shakes off her wonted firmness. Ah! how dark
Thy long-extended realms, and rueful wastes,
Where naught but silence reigns, and night, dark night,
Dark as was Chaos, ere the infant sun
Was rolled together, or had tried his beams
Athwart the gloom profound! The sickly taper,
By glimmering through thy low-browed misty vaults
(Furred round with mouldy damps and ropy slime)
Lets fall a supernumerary horror,
And only serves to make thy night more irksome.
Well do I know thee by thy trusty yew,
Cheerless, unsocial plant! that loves to dwell
Midst skulls and coffins, epitaphs and worms;
Where light-heeled ghosts and visionary shades,
Beneath the wan cold moon (as fame reports)
Embodied, thick, perform their mystic rounds.
No other merriment, dull tree! is thine.
See yonder hallowed fane—the pious work
Of names once famed, now dubious or forgot,
And buried midst the wreck of things which were;
There lie interred the more illustrious dead.
The wind is up—hark! how it howls! Methinks
Till now I never heard a sound so dreary.
Doors creak, and windows clap, and night's foul bird,
Rooked in the spire, screams loud. The gloomy aisles,
Black-plastered, and hung round with shreds of 'scutcheons,
And tattered coats of arms, send back the sound
Laden with heavier airs, from the low vaults,
The mansions of the dead. Roused from their slumbers,
In grim array the grisly spectres rise,
Grin horrible, and obstinately sullen
Pass and repass, hushed as the foot of night.
Again the screech-owl shrieks—ungracious sound!
I'll hear no more; it makes one's blood run chill.

Quite round the pile, a row of reverend elms
(Coeval near with that) all ragged show,
Long lashed by the rude winds; some rift half down
Their branchless trunks; others so thin at top
That scarce two crows could lodge in the same tree.
Strange things, the neighbours say, have happened here:
Wild shrieks have issued from the hollow tombs,
Dead men have come again, and walked about,
And the great bell has tolled, unrung, untouched.
(Such tales their cheer, at wake or gossiping,
When it draws near to witching time of night.)
Oft in the lone churchyard at night I've seen,
By glimpse of moonshine chequering through the trees,
The schoolboy with his satchel in his hand,
Whistling aloud to bear his courage up,
And lightly tripping o'er the long flat stones
(With nettles skirted, and with moss o'ergrown),
That tell in homely phrase who lie below.
Sudden he starts, and hears, or thinks he hears,
The sound of something purring at his heels;
Full fast he flies, and dares not look behind him,
Till out of breath he overtakes his fellows;
Who gather round, and wonder at the tale
Of horrid apparition, tall and ghastly,
That walks at dead of night, or takes his stand
O'er some new-opened grave, and (strange to tell!)
Evanishes at crowing of the cock.

Robert Blair

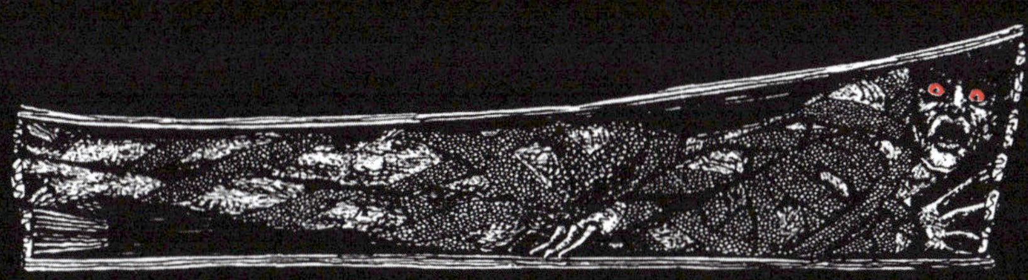

The Book of Thel (extract)

The eternal gates' terrific porter lifted the northern bar:
Thel enter'd in & saw the secrets of the land unknown.
She saw the couches of the dead, & where the fibrous roots
Of every heart on earth infixes deep its restless twists:
A land of sorrows & of tears where never smile was seen.

She wanderd in the land of clouds thro' valleys dark, listning
Dolors & lamentations; waiting oft beside a dewy grave,
She stood in silence, listning to the voices of the ground,
Till to her own grave plot she came, & there she sat down,
And heard this voice of sorrow breathèd from the hollow pit:

"Why cannot the Ear be closed to its own destruction?
Or the glistning Eye to the poison of a smile?
Why are Eyelids stord with arrows ready drawn,
Where a thousand fighting men in ambush lie?
Or an Eye of gifts & graces, show'ring fruits & coinèd gold?
Why a Tongue impress'd with honey from every wind?
Why an Ear, a whirlpool fierce to draw creations in?
Why a Nostril wide inhaling terror, trembling & affright?
Why a tender curb upon the youthful burning boy?
Why a little curtain of flesh on the bed of our desire?"

The Virgin started from her seat, & with a shriek
Fled back unhinderd till she came into the vales of Har.

William Blake

Netley Abbey: Midnight (extract)

Within the sheltered centre of the aisle,
 Beneath the ash whose growth romantic spreads
Its foliage trembling o'er the funeral pile,
 And all around a deeper darkness sheds;
While through yon arch, where the thick ivy twines,
Bright on the silvered tower the moonbeam shines,
 And the grey cloister's roofless length illumes,
Upon the mossy stone I lie reclined,
And to a visionary world resigned
 Call the pale spectres forth from the forgotten tombs.

Spirits! the desolated wreck that haunt,
 Who frequent by the village maiden seen
When sudden shouts at eve the wanderer daunt,
 And shapeless shadows sweep along the green;
And ye, in midnight horrors heard to yell
Round the destroyer of the holy cell,
 With interdictions dread of boding sound;
Who, when he prowled the rifled walls among,
Prone on his brow the massy fragment flung;—
 Come from your viewless caves, and tread this hallowed ground!

William Sotheby

Incantation

When the leaves, by thousands thinned,
A thousand times have whirled in the wind,
And the moon, with hollow cheek,
Staring from her hollow height,
Consolation seems to seek
From the dim, reechoing night;
And the fog-streaks dead and white
Lie like ghosts of lost delight
O'er highest earth and lowest sky;
Then, Autumn, work thy witchery!

Strew the ground with poppy-seeds,
And let my bed be hung with weeds,
Growing gaunt and rank and tall,
Drooping o'er me like a pall.
Send thy stealthy, white-eyed mist
Across my brow to turn and twist
Fold on fold, and leave me blind
To all save visions in the mind.
Then, in the depth of rain-fed streams
I shall slumber, and in dreams
Slide through some long glen that burns
With a crust of blood-red ferns
And brown-withered wings of brake
Like a burning lava-lake;—
So, urged to fearful, faster flow
By the awful gasp, "Hahk! hahk!" of the crow,
Shall pass by many a haunted rood
Of the nutty, odorous wood;
Or, where the hemlocks lean and loom,
Shall fill my heart with bitter gloom;
Till, lured by light, reflected cloud,
I burst aloft my watery shroud,
And upward through the ether sail
Far above the shrill wind's wail;—
But, falling thence, my soul involve
With the dust dead flowers dissolve;

And, gliding out at last to sea,
Lulled to a long tranquillity,
The perfect poise of seasons keep
With the tides that rest at neap.
So must be fulfilled the rite
That giveth me the dead year's might;
And at dawn I shall arise
A spirit, though with human eyes,
A human form and human face;
And where'er I go or stay,
There the summer's perished grace
Shall be with me, night and day.

George Parsons Lathrop

The Apparition

Convulsions came; and, where the field
    Long slept in pastoral green,
A goblin-mountain was upheaved
(Sure the scared sense was all deceived),
    Marl-glen and slag-ravine.

The unreserve of Ill was there,
    The clinkers in her last retreat;
But, ere the eye could take it in,
Or mind could comprehension win,
    It sunk!—and at our feet.

So, then, Solidity's a crust—
    The core of fire below;
All may go well for many a year,
But who can think without a fear
    Of horrors that happen so?

Herman Melville

Amor Mundi

"Oh where are you going with your love-locks flowing
On the west wind blowing along this valley track?"
"The downhill path is easy, come with me an it please ye,
We shall escape the uphill by never turning back."

So they two went together in glowing August weather,
The honey-breathing heather lay to their left and right;
And dear she was to dote on, her swift feet seemed to float on
The air like soft twin pigeons too sportive to alight.

"Oh what is that in heaven where gray cloud-flakes are seven,
Where blackest clouds hang riven just at the rainy skirt?"
"Oh that's a meteor sent us, a message dumb, portentous,
An undeciphered solemn signal of help or hurt."

"Oh what is that glides quickly where velvet flowers grow thickly,
Their scent comes rich and sickly?"—"A scaled and hooded worm."
"Oh what's that in the hollow, so pale I quake to follow?"
"Oh that's a thin dead body which waits the eternal term."

"Turn again, O my sweetest,—turn again, false and fleetest:
This beaten way thou beatest I fear is hell's own track."
"Nay, too steep for hill-mounting; nay, too late for cost-counting:
This downhill path is easy, but there's no turning back."

Christina Rossetti

The Fairies

Up the airy mountain,
Down the rushy glen,
We daren't go a-hunting
For fear of little men;
Wee folk, good folk,
Trooping all together;
Green jacket, red cap,
And white owl's feather!

Down along the rocky shore
Some make their home,
They live on crispy pancakes
Of yellow tide-foam;
Some in the reeds
Of the black mountain lake,
With frogs for their watch-dogs,
All night awake.

High on the hill-top
The old King sits;
He is now so old and grey
He's nigh lost his wits.
With a bridge of white mist
Columbkill he crosses,
On his stately journeys
From Slieveleague to Rosses;
Or going up with music
On cold starry nights,
To sup with the Queen
Of the gay Northern Lights.

They stole little Bridget
For seven years long;
When she came down again
Her friends were all gone.
They took her lightly back,
Between the night and morrow,
They thought that she was fast asleep,
But she was dead with sorrow.
They have kept her ever since
Deep within the lake,
On a bed of flag-leaves,
Watching till she wake.

By the craggy hill-side,
Through the mosses bare,
They have planted thorn-trees
For pleasure here and there.
Is any man so daring
As dig them up in spite,
He shall find their sharpest thorns
In his bed at night.

Up the airy mountain,
Down the rushy glen,
We daren't go a-hunting
For fear of little men;
Wee folk, good folk,
Trooping all together;
Green jacket, red cap,
And white owl's feather!

William Allingham

The Fairy Thorn

"Get up, our Anna dear, from the weary spinning wheel;
For your father's on the hill, and your mother is asleep:
Come up above the crags, and we'll dance a highland reel
Around the fairy thorn on the steep."

At Anna Grace's door 'twas thus the maidens cried,
Three merry maidens fair in kirtles of the green;
And Anna laid the rock and the weary wheel aside,
The fairest of the four, I ween.

They're glancing through the glimmer of the quiet eve,
Away in milky wavings of neck and ankle bare;
The heavy-sliding stream in its sleepy song they leave,
And the crags in the ghostly air:

And linking hand in hand, and singing as they go,
The maids along the hill-side have ta'en their fearless way,
Till they come to where the rowan trees in lonely beauty grow
Beside the Fairy Hawthorn grey.

The Hawthorn stands between the ashes tall and slim,
Like matron with her twin grand-daughters at her knee;
The rowan berries cluster o'er her low head grey and dim
In ruddy kisses sweet to see.

The merry maidens four have ranged them in a row,
Between each lovely couple a stately rowan stem,
And away in mazes wavy, like skimming birds they go,
Oh, never carolled bird like them!

But solemn is the silence of the silvery haze
That drinks away their voices in echoless repose,
And dreamily the evening has stilled the haunted braes,
And dreamier the gloaming grows.

And sinking one by one, like lark-notes from the sky
When the falcon's shadow saileth across the open shaw,
Are hushed the maidens' voices, as cowering down they lie
In the flutter of their sudden awe.

For, from the air above, and the grassy ground beneath,
And from the mountain-ashes and the old Whitethorn between,
A power of faint enchantment doth through their beings breathe,
And they sink down together on the green.

They sink together silent, and stealing side to side,
They fling their lovely arms o'er their drooping necks so fair,
Then vainly strive again their naked arms to hide,
For their shrinking necks again are bare.

Thus clasped and prostrate all, with their heads together bowed,
Soft o'er their bosoms beating — the only human sound —
They hear the silky footsteps of the silent fairy crowd,
Like a river in the air, gliding round.

No scream can any raise, no prayer can any say,
But wild, wild, the terror of the speechless three —
For they feel fair Anna Grace drawn silently away,
By whom they dare not look to see.

They feel their tresses twine with her parting locks of gold,
And the curls elastic falling, as her head withdraws;
They feel her sliding arms from their trancèd arms unfold,
But they may not look to see the cause:

For heavy on their senses the faint enchantment lies
Through all that night of anguish and perilous amaze;
And neither fear nor wonder can ope their quivering eyes
Or their limbs from the cold ground raise,

Till out of Night the Earth has rolled her dewy side,
With every haunted mountain and streamy vale below;
When, as the mist dissolves in the yellow morning-tide,
The maidens' trance dissolveth so.

Then fly the ghastly three as swiftly as they may,
And tell their tale of sorrow to anxious friends in vain —
They pined away and died within the year and day,
And ne'er was Anna Grace seen again.

Samuel Ferguson

Earwig Country

The flowers are white cups, poised upright,
as if waiting to be filled. Bindweed stems
hold them up to the light, like fine porcelain.

I investigated them for scent. A flower like that
must be an olfactory delight, but deep within
dark brown clawed things crawled.

As children we believed earwigs aimed
to enter our heads through the portal
of our ears, bury themselves in our brains.

Beautiful things have inner horrors
I learned to be wary of. The hedges held aloft
whole tea services of bone china, pure white

full of the plotting of earwigs. Put your ear
too close and you will hear them, whispering
in their marble citadels. They are coming for us still.

Angela Topping

Spellbound

The night is D A R K E N I N G round me,
The *wild* winds coldly B L O W;
But a tyrant spell has ***bound*** me
And I cannot, cannot go.

The giant trees are ***bending***
Their B A R E B O U G H S weighed with snow.
And the storm is *fast* DESCENDING,
And yet I cannot go.

Clouds ***beyond*** clouds above me,
Wastes beyond W A S T E S below;
But N O T H I N G drear can ***move me***;
I will not, cannot go.

Emily Brontë

Her Vision in the Wood

Dry timber under that rich foliage,
At wine-dark midnight in the sacred wood,
Too old for a man's love I stood in rage
Imagining men. Imagining that I could
A greater with a lesser pang assuage
Or but to find if withered vein ran blood,
I tore my body that its wine might cover
Whatever could recall the lip of lover.

And after that I held my fingers up,
Stared at the wine-dark nail, or dark that ran
Down every withered finger from the top;
But the dark changed to red, and torches shone,
And deafening music shook the leaves; a troop
Shouldered a litter with a wounded man,
Or smote upon the string and to the sound
Sang of the beast that gave the fatal wound.

All stately women moving to a song
With loosened hair or foreheads grief-distraught,
It seemed a Quattrocento painter's throng,
A thoughtless image of Mantegna's thought—
Why should they think that are for ever young?
Till suddenly in grief's contagion caught,
I stared upon his blood-bedabbled breast
And sang my malediction with the rest.

That thing all blood and mire, that beast-torn wreck,
Half turned and fixed a glazing eye on mine,
And, though love's bitter-sweet had all come back,
Those bodies from a picture or a coin
Nor saw my body fall nor heard it shriek,
Nor knew, drunken with singing as with wine,
That they had brought no fabulous symbol there
But my heart's victim and its torturer.

W. B. Yeats

The Pilgrimage to Paradise (extract)

When, passing on, they fell into a wood,
A thicket full of brambles, thorns and briars;
A graceless grove, that never did man good,
But wretched endings of the world's desires;
Where snakes and adders, and such venomed things,
Had slain a number with their cruel stings.

Some metamorphosed like Actaeon were,
Diana smiling at their lewd desires;
Some semitawres, and some more half a bear,
Other half swine, deep wallowing in the mires:
All beastly minds, that could not be reformed,
Were to the shapes of their own same transformed.

There might he see the satyrs in their dances,
Half men, half beasts, or devils in their kinds;
There might he see the Muses, in their trances,
Lie down as dead, as if they had no minds;
There might he see, in all, so little good,
As made him wish he had been through the wood.

Nicholas Breton

The Witches' Wood

There was a wood, a witches' wood,
All the trees therein were pale.
They bore no branches green and good,
But as it were a gray nun's veil.

They talked and chattered in the wind
From morning dawn to set of sun,
Like men and women that have sinned,
Whose thousand evil tongues are one.

Their roots were like the hands of men,
Grown hard and brown with clutching gold.
Their foliage women's tresses when
The hair is withered, thin, and old.

There never did a sweet bird sing
For happy love about his nest.
The clustered bats on evil wing
Each hollow trunk and bough possessed.

And in the midst a pool there lay
Of water white, as tho' a scare
Had frightened off the eye of day
And kept the Moon reflected there.

Mary Coleridge

Grotesque

Why do the lilies goggle their tongues at me
When I pluck them;
And writhe, and twist,
And strangle themselves against my fingers,
So that I can hardly weave the garland
For your hair?
Why do they shriek your name
And spit at me
When I would cluster them?
Must I kill them
To make them lie still,
And send you a wreath of lolling corpses
To turn putrid and soft
On your forehead
While you dance?

Amy Lowell

Haunted Spot

The close-twined branches interlock o'erhead,
'Twixt leaf and leaf no ray, no glimpse of blue;
From the live roof is gray-green twilight shed,
Heavily clings at noon the dull chill dew;
The snake-like roots of the large trees break through
The black, moist sod; rank weeds spread everywhere,
Damp shadow and mirk vapors fill the air.

A yellowish pool hath slowly filtered here
From drip and ooze and frequent wash of rains:
No lapse of living waters greets the ear,
Thick crust of slime its sluggish surface stains.
Here Silence dwells – a vague, wild terror gains
The soul before this mystery divine,
Evil in action, evil in design.

The poisoned flower hath overwrought the brain,
The wood seems peopled with strange images,
Huge forms uncouth in slow, unending trains,
Life's terrors and its nameless miseries,
Now like a sullen mist between the trees,
Now close and threatening, distinct and near,
While hateful discords grate upon the ear.

Sin, madness, poverty, disease and age,
And halting last, the unmixed evil, death.
How near to her they come, life's heritage
Of ancient ills! No outlet openeth:
Her wild cry echoes far above, beneath,
Fills the thick air with trouble, wanes and dies,
Meeting the hollow earth and empty skies.

Emma Lazarus

The Weird Gathering (extract)

Nay, look not down that lighted dell,
Thou startled traveller!—
Thy christian eye should never dwell
On gaunt, grey witch and fiend of hell
And evil Trumpeter!
But, the traveller turned him from his way,
For he heard the revelling—
And saw the red light's wizard ray
Among the dark leafed branches play,
Like an unholy thing.
He knelt him on the rocks, and cast,
A fearful glance beneath,—
Wizard and hag before him passed,
Each wilder, fiercer than the last,—
His heart grew cold as death!

John Greenleaf Whittier

The Haunted Oak

Pray why are you so bare, so bare,
Oh, bough of the old oak-tree;
And why, when I go through the shade you throw,
Runs a shudder over me?

My leaves were green as the best, I trow,
And sap ran free in my veins,
But I saw in the moonlight dim and weird
A guiltless victim's pains.

I bent me down to hear his sigh;
I shook with his gurgling moan,
And I trembled sore when they rode away,
And left him here alone.

They'd charged him with the old, old crime,
And set him fast in jail:
Oh, why does the dog howl all night long,
And why does the night wind wail?

He prayed his prayer and he swore his oath,
And he raised his hand to the sky;
But the beat of hoofs smote on his ear,
And the steady tread drew nigh.

Who is it rides by night, by night,
Over the moonlit road?
And what is the spur that keeps the pace,
What is the galling goad?

And now they beat at the prison door,
"Ho, keeper, do not stay!
We are friends of him whom you hold within,
And we fain would take him away

"From those who ride fast on our heels
With mind to do him wrong;
They have no care for his innocence,
And the rope they bear is long."

They have fooled the jailer with lying words,
They have fooled the man with lies;
The bolts unbar, the locks are drawn,
And the great door open flies.

Now they have taken him from the jail,
And hard and fast they ride,
And the leader laughs low down in his throat,
As they halt my trunk beside.

Oh, the judge, he wore a mask of black,
And the doctor one of white,
And the minister, with his oldest son,
Was curiously bedight.

Oh, foolish man, why weep you now?
'Tis but a little space,
And the time will come when these shall dread
The mem'ry of your face.

I feel the rope against my bark,
And the weight of him in my grain,
I feel in the throe of his final woe
The touch of my own last pain.

And never more shall leaves come forth
On the bough that bears the ban;
I am burned with dread, I am dried and dead,
From the curse of a guiltless man.

And ever the judge rides by, rides by,
And goes to hunt the deer,
And ever another rides his soul
In the guise of a mortal fear.

And ever the man he rides me hard,
And never a night stays he;
For I feel his curse as a haunted bough,
On the trunk of a haunted tree.

Paul Laurence Dunbar

Dreams in War Time (extract)

II

I dug a grave under an oak-tree.
With infinite care, I stamped my spade
Into the heavy grass.
The sod sucked it,
And I drew it out with effort,
Watching the steel run liquid in the moonlight
As it became clear.
I stooped, and dug, and never turned,
For behind me,
On the dried leaves,
My own face lay like a white pebble,
Waiting.

V

I followed a procession of singing girls
Who danced to the glitter of tambourines.
Where the street turned at a lighted corner,
I caught the purple dress of one of the dancers,
But, as I grasped it, it tore,
And the purple dye ran from it
Like blood
Upon the ground.

Amy Lowell

The Watcher in the Woods

Deep in the wood's recesses cool
I see the fairy dancers glide,
In cloth of gold, in gown of green,
My lord and lady side by side.

But who has hung from leaf to leaf,
From flower to flower, a silken twine –
A cloud of grey that holds the dew
In globes of clear enchanted wine?

Or stretches far from branch to branch,
From thorn to thorn, in diamond rain,
Who caught the cup of crystal pure
And hung so fair the shining chain?

'Tis death, the spider, in his net,
Who lures the dancers as they glide,
In cloth of gold, in gown of green,
My lord and lady side by side.

Dora Sigerson Shorter

A Musical Instrument

What was he doing, the great god Pan,
Down in the reeds by the river?
Spreading ruin and scattering ban,
Splashing and paddling with hoofs of a goat,
And breaking the golden lilies afloat
With the dragon-fly on the river.

He tore out a reed, the great god Pan,
From the deep cool bed of the river;
The limpid water turbidly ran,
And the broken lilies a-dying lay,
And the dragon-fly had fled away,
Ere he brought it out of the river.

High on the shore sat the great god Pan,
While turbidly flow'd the river;
And hack'd and hew'd as a great god can
With his hard bleak steel at the patient reed,
Till there was not a sign of the leaf indeed
To prove it fresh from the river.

He cut it short, did the great god Pan
(How tall it stood in the river!),
Then drew the pith, like the heart of a man,
Steadily from the outside ring,
And notch'd the poor dry empty thing
In holes, as he sat by the river.

'This is the way,' laugh'd the great god Pan
(Laugh'd while he sat by the river),
'The only way, since gods began
To make sweet music, they could succeed.'
Then dropping his mouth to a hole in the reed,
He blew in power by the river.

Sweet, sweet, sweet, O Pan!
Piercing sweet by the river!
Blinding sweet, O great god Pan!
The sun on the hill forgot to die,
And the lilies revived, and the dragon-fly
Came back to dream on the river.

Yet half a beast is the great god Pan,
To laugh as he sits by the river,
Making a poet out of a man:
The true gods sigh for the cost and pain—
For the reed which grows nevermore again
As a reed with the reeds of the river.

Elizabeth Barrett Browning

Children of the Mist

The cold airs from the river creep
About the murky town,
The spectral willows, half asleep,
Trail their thin tresses down
Where the dim tide goes wandering slow,
Sad with perpetual ebb and flow.

The great blind river, cold and wide,
Goes groping by the shore,
And still where water and land divide
He murmurs evermore
The overword of an old song,
The echo of an ancient wrong.

There is no sound 'twixt stream and sky,
But white mists walk the strand,
Waifs of the night that wander by,
Wraiths from the river-land –
While here, beneath the dripping trees,
Stray other souls more lost than these.

Voiceless and visionless they fare,
Known all too well to me –
Ghosts of the years that never were,
The years that could not be –
And still, beneath the eternal skies
The old blind river gropes and sighs.

Rosamund Marriott Watson

Childe Roland to the Dark Tower Came (extract)

XIX

A sudden little river crossed my path,
    As unexpected as a serpent comes,
    No sluggish tide congenial to the glooms;
This, as it frothed by, might have been a bath
For the fiend's glowing hoof – to see the wrath
    Of its black eddy bespate with flukes and spumes.

XX

So petty yet so spiteful! All along,
    Low scrubby alders kneeled down over it;
    Drenched willows flung them headlong in a fit
Of mute despair, a suicidal throng:
The river, which had done them all the wrong,
    Whate'er that was, rolled by, deterred no whit.

XXI

Which, while I forded, – good saints, how I feared
    To set my foot upon a dead man's cheek,
    Each step, or feel the spear I thrust to seek
For hollows, tangled in his hair or beard!
It may have been a water-rat I speared,
    But, ugh!, it sounded like a baby's shriek.

Robert Browning

East River

Dour river
Jaded with monotony of lights
Diving off mast heads....
Lights mad with creating in a river... turning its sullen back....
Heave up, river...
Vomit back into the darkness your spawn of light...
The night will gut what you give her.

Lola Ridge

Brooklyn Bridge

Pythoness body – arching
Over the night like an ecstasy –
I feel your coils tightening...
And the world's lessening breath.

Lola Ridge

Christ Church, Oxford Night

Faint from the bell the ghastly echoes fall,
    That grates within the grey cathedral tower –
Let me not enter through the portal tall,
    Lest the strange spirit of the moonless hour
Should give a life to those pale people, who
Lie in their fretted niches, two and two –
Each with his head on pillowy stone reposed,
And his hands lifted, and his eyelids closed.

A cold and starless vapour, through the night,
    Moves as the paleness of corruption passes
Over a corpse's features, like a light
    That half illumines what it most effaces;
The calm round water gazes on the sky,
Like the reflection of the lifeless eye
Of one who sleep and dreams of being slain,
Struggling in frozen frenzy, and in vain.

From many a mouldering oriel, as to flout,
    Its pale, grave brow of ivy-tressèd stone,
Comes the incongruous laugh, and revel shout —
    Above, some solitary casement, thrown
Wide open to the wavering night wind,
Admits its chill – so deathful, yet so kind
Unto the fevered brow and fiery eye
Of one, whose night hour passeth sleeplessly.

Ye melancholy chambers! I could shun
    The darkness of your silence, with such fear,
As places where slow murder had been done.
    How many noble spirits have died here –
Withering away in yearnings to aspire,
Gnawed by mocked hope — devoured by their own fire!
Methinks the grave must feel a colder bed
To spirits such as these, than unto common dead.

John Ruskin

In the City of Night

City of night,
Wrap me in your folds of shadow.

City of twilight,
City that projects into the west,
City whose columns rest upon the sunset, city of square, threatening masses blocking out the light:
City of twilight,
Wrap me in your folds of shadow.

City of midnight, city that the full moon overflows, city where the cats prowl and the closed iron dust-carts go rattling through the shadows:
City of midnight,
Wrap me in your folds of shadow.

City of early morning, cool fresh-sprinkled city, city whose sharp roof peaks are splintered against the stars, city that unbars tall haggard gates in pity,
City of midnight,
Wrap me in your folds of shadow.

City of rain, city where the bleak wind batters the hard drops once and again, sousing a shivering, cursing beggar who clings amid the stiff Apostles on the cathedral portico;
City where the glare is dull and lowering, city where the clouds flare and flicker as they pass upwards, where sputtering lamps stare into the muddy pools beneath them;
City where the winds shriek up the streets and tear into the squares, city whose cobbles quiver and whose pinnacles waver before the buzzing chatter of raindrops in their flight;
City of midnight,
Drench me with your rain of sorrow.

City of vermilion curtains, city whose windows drip with crimson, tawdry, tinselled, sensual city, throw me pitilessly into your crowds.
City filled with women's faces leering at the passers by,
City with doorways always open, city of silks and swishing laces, city where bands bray dance-music all night in the plaza,
City where the overscented light hangs tepidly, stabbed with jabber of the crowd, city where the stars stare coldly, falsely smiling through the smoke-filled air,
City of midnight,
Smite me with your despair.

City of emptiness, city of the white façades, city where one lonely dangling lantern wavers aloft like a taper before a marble sarcophagus, frightening away the ghosts;
City where a single white-lit window in a motionless blackened house-front swallows the hosts of darkness that stream down the street towards it;
City above whose dark tree-tangled park emerges suddenly, unlit, uncannily, a grey ghostly tower whose base is lost in the fog, and whose summit has no end.
City of midnight,
Bury me in your silence.

City of night,
Wrap me in your folds of shadow.

City of restlessness, city where I have tramped and wandered,
City where the herded crowds glance at me suspiciously, city where the churches are locked, the shops unopened, the houses without hospitality,
City of restlessness,
Wrap me in your folds of shadow.

City of sleeplessness, city of cheap airless rooms, where in the gloom are heard snores through the partition, lovers that struggle, couples that squabble, cabs that rattle, cats that squall,
City of sleeplessness,
Wrap me in your folds of shadow.

City of feverish dreams, city that is being besieged by all the demons of darkness, city of innumerable shadowy vaults and towers, city where passion flowers desperately and treachery ends in death the strong:
City of night,
Wrap me in your folds of shadow.

John Gould Fletcher

The Harlot's House

We caught the tread of dancing feet,
We loitered down the moonlit street,
And stopped beneath the Harlot's house.

Inside, above the din and fray,
We heard the loud musicians play
The "Treues Liebes Herz" of Strauss.

Like strange mechanical grotesques,
Making fantastic arabesques,
The shadows raced across the blind.

We watched the ghostly dancers spin
To sound of horn and violin,
Like black leaves wheeling in the wind.

Like wire-pulled automatons,
Slim silhouetted skeletons
Went sidling through the slow quadrille,

Then took each other by the hand,
And danced a stately saraband;
Their laughter echoed thin and shrill.

Sometimes a clockwork puppet pressed
A phantom lover to her breast,
Sometimes they seemed to try to sing.

Sometimes a horrible marionette
Came out, and smoked its cigarette
Upon the steps like a live thing.

Then turning to my love I said,
"The dead are dancing with the dead,
The dust is whirling with the dust."

But she, she heard the violin,
And left my side, and entered in;
Love passed into the house of Lust.

Then suddenly the tune went false,
The dancers wearied of the waltz,
The shadows ceased to wheel and whirl,

And down the long and silent street,
The dawn, with silver-sandaled feet,
Crept like a frightened girl.

Oscar Wilde

Flotsam (extract)

Crass rays streaming from the vestibules;
Cafes glittering like jeweled teeth;
High-flung signs
Blinking yellow phosphorescent eyes;
Girls in black
Circling monotonously
About the orange lights...

Nothing to guess at...
Save the darkness above
Crouching like a great cat.

In the dim-lit square,
Where disheveled trees
Tustle with the wind—the wind like a scythe
Mowing their last leaves
Arcs shimmering through a greenish haze—
Pale oval arcs
Like ailing virgins,
Each out of a halo circumscribed,
Pallidly staring...

Lola Ridge

Beyond the Last Lamp

While rain, with eve in partnership,
Descended darkly, drip, drip, drip,
Beyond the last lone lamp I passed
    Walking slowly, whispering sadly,
    Two linked loiterers, wan, downcast:
Some heavy thought constrained each face,
And blinded them to time and place.

The pair seemed lovers, yet absorbed
In mental scenes no longer orbed
By love's young rays. Each countenance
    As it slowly, as it sadly
    Caught the lamplight's yellow glance
Held in suspense a misery
At things which had been or might be.

When I retrod that watery way
Some hours beyond the droop of day,
Still I found pacing there the twain
    Just as slowly, just as sadly,
    Heedless of the night and rain.
One could but wonder who they were
And what wild woe detained them there.

Though thirty years of blur and blot
Have slid since I beheld that spot,
And saw in curious converse there
    Moving slowly, moving sadly
    That mysterious tragic pair,
Its olden look may linger on -
All but the couple; they have gone.

Whither? Who knows, indeed ... And yet
To me, when nights are weird and wet,
Without those comrades there at tryst
    Creeping slowly, creeping sadly,
    That lone lane does not exist.
There they seem brooding on their pain,
And will, while such a lane remain.

Thomas Hardy

London

I wander thro' each charter'd street,
Near where the charter'd Thames does flow,
And mark in every face I meet
Marks of weakness, marks of woe.

In every cry of every man,
In every Infant's cry of fear,
In every voice, in every ban,
The mind-forg'd manacles I hear.

How the Chimney-sweeper's cry
Every blackning Church appalls,
And the hapless Soldier's sigh
Runs in blood down Palace walls.

But most thro' midnight streets I hear
How the youthful Harlot's curse
Blasts the new-born Infant's tear,
And blights with plagues the Marriage hearse.

William Blake

November

Dim mist of a fog-bound day ...
From the lilac trees that droop in St Mary's Square
The dead leaves fall, a silent, shivering, cloud.
Through the grey haze the carts loom heavy, gigantic
Down the dull street. Children at play in the gutter
Quarrel and cry; their voices sound flat and toneless.
With a sound like the shuffling tread of some giant monster
I hear the trains escape from the stations near, and tear their way
    into the country.
Everything looks fantastic, repellent, I see from my window
And old man pass, dull, formless, like the stump of a dead tree moving.
The virginia creeper, like blood, streams down the face of the houses ...
Even the railings, blackened and sharply defined, look evil and
    strangely malignant.
... Dim Mist of a fog-bound day,
From the lilac trees that droop in St Mary's Square
The dead leaves fall, a silent, fluttering crowd —
Dead leaves that shivering fall on the barren earth.
... Over and under it all, the muttering murmur of London.

Katherine Mansfield

On Receiving the First News of the War

Snow is a strange white word;
No ice or frost
Has asked of bud or bird
For Winter's cost.

Yet ice and frost and snow
From earth to sky
This Summer land doth know;
No man knows why.

In all men's hearts it is:
Some spirit old
Hath turned with malign kiss
Our lives to mould.

Red fangs have torn His face.
God's blood is shed:
He mourns from His lone place
His children dead.

O ancient crimson curse!
Corrode, consume;
Give back this universe
Its pristine bloom.

Isaac Rosenberg

The Ascent of Man (extract)

War rages on the teeming earth;
    The hot and sanguinary fight
Begins with each new creature's birth:
    A dreadful war where might is right;
Where still the strongest slay and win,
Where weakness is the only sin.

There is no truce to this drawn battle,
    Which ends but to begin again;
The drip of blood, the hoarse death-rattle,
    The roar of rage, the shriek of pain,
Are rife in fairest grove and dell,
Turning earth's flowery haunts to hell.

Mathilde Blind

The Shadow

There was a shadow on the moon; I saw it poise and tilt, and go
Its lonely way, and so I know that the blue velvet night will soon
Blaze loud and bright, as if the stars were crashing right into the town,
And tumbling streets and houses down, and smashing people like wine-jars ...

Fear wakes:
What then?
Strayed shadow of the Fear that breaks
The world's young men.

Bright fingers point all round the sky; they point and grope and cannot find.
(God's hand, you'd think, and he gone blind.) ... The queer white faces twist and cry.
Last time they came they messed our square, and left it a hot rubbish-heap,
With people sunk in it so deep, you could not even hear them swear.

Fire blinds.
What then?
Pale shadows of the Pain that grinds
The worlds young men.

The weak blood running down the street, oh, does it run like fire, like wine?
Are the spilt brains so keen, so fine, crushed limbs so swift, dead dreams so sweet?
There is a Plain where limbs and dreams and brains to set the world a-fire
Lie tossed in sodden heaps of mire ... Crash! Tonight's show begins, it seems.

Death ... Well,
What then?
Rim of the shadow of the Hell
Of the world's young men.

Rose Macaulay

London in War

White faces,
Like helpless petals on the stream,
Swirl by,
Or linger
And then go ...

Ancient summer burns
Where green trees branch
From palaces of stone;
I see the brightness
Through a throbbing gloom,
While a death rattles
To a tripping melody ...

Hot laughter comes,
With tears of ice,
Where War is God
And God is War;
For He has torn
The gallant spirits that He gave,
Till joy is agony,
And agony is joy ...

Night falls with its olden touch,
But sleep comes
Like a bloody man,
And the stars
Are wounded birds
That fall
For ever ...

Helen Dircks

Doomsday

The end of everything approaches;
I hear it coming
Loud as the wheels of painted coaches
On turnpikes drumming;
Loud as the pomp of plumy hearses,
Or pennoned charges;
Loud as when every oar reverses
Venetian barges;
Loud as the caves of covered bridges
Fulfilled with rumble
Of hooves; and loud as cloudy ridges
When glaciers tumble;
Like creeping thunder this continues
Diffused and distant,
Loud in our ears and in our sinews,
Insane, insistent;
Loud as a lion scorning carrion
Further and further;
Loud as the ultimate loud clarion
Or the first murther.

Elinor Wylie

The City of Dreadful Night (extract)

II

As I came through the desert thus it was,
As I came through the desert: Eyes of fire
Glared at me throbbing with a starved desire;
The hoarse and heavy and carnivorous breath
Was hot upon me from deep jaws of death;
Sharp claws, swift talons, fleshless fingers cold
Plucked at me from the bushes, tried to hold:
But I strode on austere;
No hope could have no fear.

III

As I came through the desert thus it was,
As I came through the desert: Lo you, there,
That hillock burning with a brazen glare;
Those myriad dusky flames with points a-glow
Which writhed and hissed and darted to and fro;
A Sabbath of the Serpents, heaped pell-mell
For Devil's roll-call and some *fête* of Hell:
Yet I strode on austere;
No hope could have no fear.

VI

As I came through the desert thus it was,
As I came through the desert: On the left
The sun arose and crowned a broad crag-cleft;
There stopped and burned out black, except a rim,
A bleeding eyeless socket, red and dim;
Whereon the moon fell suddenly south-west,
And stood above the right-hand cliffs at rest:
Still I strode on austere;
No hope could have no fear.

James Thomson

Petron (extract)

III

In the midst of a ravaged city, the returned exile stands by the ruins of his ancient home. The blood of his slaughtered father has long been washed away by the rains, all traces of habitation have long been obliterated, and nothing remains but a heap of shattered stones where the lizards dart and snakes find shelter.

Searching among the rubble, he finds a battered toy that was once his own, but even as he holds it, it stirs in his hand and becomes a grasshopper, then an old man, a monstrous spider, a woman's breast, a bunch of faded grass, a little heap of bones and so to a lizard which eludes his grasp, and darts away among the sunlit stones.

Hugh Sykes Davies

Overheard on a Saltmarsh

Nymph, nymph, what are your beads?

Green glass, goblin. Why do you stare at them?

Give them me.

No.

Give them me. Give them me.

No.

Then I will howl all night in the reeds,
Lie in the mud and howl for them.

Goblin, why do you love them so?

They are better than stars or water,
Better than voices of winds that sing,
Better than any man's fair daughter,
Your green glass beads on a silver ring.

Hush, I stole them out of the moon.

Give me your beads, I want them.

No.

I will howl in the deep lagoon
For your green glass beads. I love them so.
Give them me. Give them.

No.

Harold Monro

The Hills of Ruel

"Over the hills and far away" —
That is the tune I heard one day
When heather-drowsy I lay and listened
And watched where the stealthy sea-tide glistened.
Beside me there on the Hills of Ruel
An old man stooped and gathered fuel —
And I asked him this: if his son were dead,
As the folk in Glendaruel all said,
How could he still believe that never
Duncan had crossed the shadowy river.
Forth from his breast the old man drew
A lute that once on a rowan-tree grew:
And, speaking no words, began to play
"Over the hills and far away."
"But how do you know," I said, thereafter,
"That Duncan has heard the fairy laughter?
How do you know he has followed the cruel
Honey-sweet folk of the Hills of Ruel?"
"How do I know?" the old man said,
"Sure I know well my boy's not dead:
For late on the morrow they hid him, there
Where the black earth moistens his yellow hair,
I saw him alow on the moor close by,
I watched him low on the hillside lie,
An' I heard him laughin' wild up there,
An' talk, talk, talkin' beneath his hair —
For down o'er his face his long hair lay
But I saw it was cold and ashy grey.
Ay, laughin' and talkin' wild he was,
An' that to a Shadow out on the grass,
A Shadow that made my blood go chill,
For never its like have I seen on the hill.
An' the moon came up, and the stars grew white,
An' the hills grew black in the bloom o' the night,
An' I watched till the death-star sank in the moon
And the moonmaid fled with her flittermice shoon,
Then the Shadow that lay on the moorside there
Rose up and shook its wildmoss hair,
And Duncan he laughed no more, but grey
As the rainy dust of a rainy day,
Went over the hills and far away."

Fiona MacLeod

The Sands of Dee

"O Mary, go and call the cattle home,
And call the cattle home,
And call the cattle home,
Across the sands of Dee."
The western wind was wild and dark with foam,
And all alone went she.

The western tide crept up along the sand,
And o'er and o'er the sand,
And round and round the sand,
As far as eye could see.
The rolling mist came down and hid the land:
And never home came she.

"O is it weed, or fish, or floating hair —
A tress of golden hair,
A drownèd maiden's hair,
Above the nets at sea?"
Was never salmon yet that shone so fair
Among the stakes on Dee.

They rowed her in across the rolling foam,
The cruel crawling foam,
The cruel hungry foam,
To her grave beside the sea.
But still the boatmen hear her call the cattle home,
Across the sands of Dee.

Charles Kingsley

The Cave of Despair

Ere long they comee, where that same wicked wight
His dwelling has, low in an hollow cave,
Farre underneath a craggie clift ypight,
Darke, dolefull, drearie, like a greedie grave,
That still for carrion carcases doth crave:
On top whereof aye dwelt the ghastly Owle,
Shrieking his balefull note, which ever drave
Farre from that haunt all other chearefull fowle;
And all about it wandring ghostes did waile and howle.

And all about old stockes and stubs of trees,
Whereon nor fruit, nor leafe was ever seene,
Did hang upon the ragged rocky knees;
On which had many wretches hanged beene,
Whose carcases were scattered on the greene,
And throwne about the cliffs. Arrived there,
That bare-head knight for dread and dolefull teene,
Would faine have fled, ne durst approchen neare,
But th'other forst him stay, and comforted in feare.

That darkesome cave they enter, where they find
That cursed man, low sitting on the ground,
Musing full sadly in his sullen mind;
His griesie lockes, long growen, and unbound,
Disordred hong about his shoulders round,
And hid his face; through which his hollow eyne
Lookt deadly dull, and stared as astound;
His raw-bone cheeks through penurie and pine
Were shronke into his jawes, as he did never dine.

His garment nought but many ragged clouts,
With thornes together pind and patched was,
The which his naked sides he wrapt abouts;
And him beside there lay upon the gras
A drearie corse, whose life away did pas,
All wallowed in his owne yet luke-warme bloode,
That from his wound yet welled fresh, alas;
In which a rustie knife fast fixed stood,
And made an open passage for the gushing flood.

Edmund Spenser

Quicksand

My love, don't let me, going to sleep
fall into the dark cave.
I fear the sucking sand
I fear the eager hollows in the water,
places with bogholes underground.

Down there there's ancient wood and bogdeal:
the Fianna's bones are there at rest
with rustless swords — and a drowned girl,
a noose around her neck.

Now there is a weak ebb-tide:
the moon is full, the sea will leave the land
and tonight when I close my eyes
let there be terra firma, let there be hard sand.

Nuala Ní Dhomhnaill

A Forsaken Garden (extract)

Here death may deal not again for ever;
    Here change may come not till all change end.
From the graves they have made they shall rise up never,
    Who have left nought living to ravage and rend.
Earth, stones, and thorns of the wild ground growing,
    While the sun and the rain live, these shall be;
Till a last wind's breath upon all these blowing
        Roll the sea.

Till the slow sea rise and the sheer cliff crumble,
    Till terrace and meadow the deep gulfs drink,
Till the strength of the waves of the high tides humble
    The fields that lessen, the rocks that shrink,
Here now in his triumph where all things falter,
    Stretched out on the spoils that his own hand spread,
As a god self-slain on his own strange altar,
        Death lies dead.

Algernon Charles Swinburne

Written in the Church Yard at Middleton in Sussex

Pressed by the moon, mute arbitress of tides,
    While the loud equinox its power combines,
    The sea no more its swelling surge confines,
But o'er the shrinking land sublimely rides.
The wild blast, rising from the western cave,
    Drives the huge billows from their heaving bed,
    Tears from their grassy tombs the village dead,
And breaks the silent sabbath of the grave!
With shells and sea-weed mingled, on the shore
    Lo! their bones whiten in the frequent wave;
    But vain to them the winds and waters rave;
They hear the warring elements no more:
While I am doomed—by life's long storm oppressed
To gaze with envy on their gloomy rest.

Charlotte Smith

A Man Adrift on a Slim Spar

A man adrift on a slim spar
A horizon smaller than the rim of a bottle
Tented waves rearing lashy dark points
The near whine of froth in circles.
God is cold.

The incessant raise and swing of the sea
And growl after growl of crest
The sinkings, green, seething, endless
The upheaval half-completed.
God is cold.

The seas are in the hollow of The Hand;
Oceans may be turned to a spray
Raining down through the stars
Because of a gesture of pity toward a babe.
Oceans may become grey ashes,
Die with a long moan and a roar
Amid the tumult of the fishes
And the cries of the ships,
Because The Hand beckons the mice.

A horizon smaller than a doomed assassin's cap,
Inky, surging tumults
A reeling, drunken sky and no sky
A pale hand sliding from a polished spar.
God is cold.

The puff of a coat imprisoning air.
A face kissing the water-death
A weary slow sway of a lost hand
And the sea, the moving sea, the sea.
God is cold.

Stephen Crane

Dirge

Prayer unsaid, and mass unsung, Deadman's dirge must still be rung:
Dingle-dong, the dead-bells sound! Mermen chant his dirge around!

Wash him bloodless, smooth him fair, Stretch his limbs, and sleek his hair
Dingle-dong, the dead-bells go! Mermen swing them to and fro!

In the wormless sand shall he Feast for no foul glutton be:
Dingle-dong, the dead-bells chime! Mermen keep the tone and time!

We must with a tombstone brave Shut the shark out from his grave
Dingle-dong, the dead-bells toll! Mermen dirgers ring his knoll!

Such a slab will we lay o'er him All the dead shall rise before him!
Dingle-dong, the dead-bells boom! Mermen lay him in his tomb!

George Darley

Sir Roland: A Fragment (extract)

Soon as the vessel cuts the foamy tide,
Around strange spectres and fell monsters glide:
One bathed in tears rose from the liquid bed,
With the soft semblance of a virgin's head,
Thrice waved her hand and shook her sedgy hair,
And heaved a piteous sigh, and cried—'Beware!'
Next came an aged seer, whose feeble breath
Could scarcely utter—'Knight, beware of death!'
Then plunging downward in a serpent's form,
They curled the surges like an angry storm.
Now thousand other grisly shapes were seen,
Rolling their fiery eyes the waves between:
Here shrieking maidens felt the forced embrace,
There Murder laughed, and showed his guilty face.
A moment after, all was hushed and o'er,
And such portentous phantoms threat no more.

Robert Merry

Youth and the Pilgrim

Gray pilgrim, you have journeyed far,
I pray you tell to me
Is there a land where Love is not,
By shore of any sea?
For I am weary of the god,
And I would flee from him
Tho' I must take a ship and go
Beyond the ocean's rim.
"I know a port where Love is not,
The ship is in your hand,
Then plunge your sword within your breast
And you will reach the land."

Sara Teasdale

The Rime of the Ancient Mariner (extract)

The western wave was all aflame.
The day was well nigh done!
Almost upon the western wave
Rested the broad bright Sun;
When that strange shape drove suddenly
Betwixt us and the Sun.

And straight the Sun was flecked with bars,
(Heaven's Mother send us grace!)
As if through a dungeon grate he peered
With broad and burning face.

Alas! (thought I, and my heart beat loud)
How fast she nears and nears!
Are those *her* sails that glance in the Sun,
Like restless gossameres?

Are those *her* ribs through which the Sun
Did peer, as through a grate?
And is that Woman all her crew?
Is that a DEATH? and are there two?
Is DEATH that woman's mate?

Her lips were red, *her* looks were free,
Her locks were yellow as gold:
Her skin was as white as leprosy,
The Nightmare LIFE-IN-DEATH was she,
Who thicks man's blood with cold.

The naked hulk alongside came,
And the twain were casting dice;
'The game is done! I've won! I've won!'
Quoth she, and whistles thrice.

The Sun's rim dips; the stars rush out:
At one stride comes the dark;
With far-heard whisper, o'er the sea,
Off shot the spectre-bark.

We listened and looked sideways up!
Fear at my heart, as at a cup,
My lifeblood seemed to sip!
The stars were dim, and thick the night,
The steersman's face by his lamp gleamed white;
From the sails the dew did drip—
Till clomb above the eastern bar
The hornèd Moon, with one bright star
Within the nether tip.

One after one, by the star-dogged Moon,
Too quick for groan or sigh,
Each turned his face with ghastly pang,
And cursed me with his eye.

Four times fifty living men,
(And I heard nor sigh nor groan)
With heavy thump, a lifeless lump,
They dropped down one by one.

The souls did from their bodies fly—
They fled to bliss or woe!
And every soul, it passed me by,
Like the whizz of my cross-bow!

Samuel Taylor Coleridge

The Sea of Death (extract)

Methought I saw
Life swiftly treading over endless space;
And, at her foot-print, but a bygone pace,
The ocean-past, which, with increasing wave,
Swallow'd her steps like a pursuing grave.
Sad were my thoughts that anchor'd silently
On the dead waters of that passionless sea,
Unstirr'd by any touch of living breath:
Silence hung over it, and drowsy Death,
Like a gorged sea-bird, slept with folded wings
On crowded carcases – sad passive things
That wore the thin grey surface, like a veil
Over the calmness of their features pale.

Thomas Hood

The Berg (A Dream)

I saw a ship of martial build
(Her standards and her brave apparel on)
Directed as by madness mere
Against a solid iceberg steer,
Nor budge it, though the infatuate ship went down.
The impact made huge ice-cubes fall
Sullen, in tons that crashed the deck;
But that one avalanche was all –
No other movement save the foundering wreck.

Along the spurs of ridges pale,
Not any slenderest shaft and frail,
A prism over glass-green gorges lone,
Toppled; or lace of traceries fine,
Nor pendant drops in grot or mine
Were jarred when the stunned ship went down.
Nor sole the gulls in cloud that wheeled
Circling one snow-flanked field afar,
But nearer fowl the floes that skimmed
And crystal beaches, felt no jar.
No thrill transmitted stirred the lock
Of jack-straw needle-ice at base;
Towers undermined by waves—the block
Atilt impending—kept their place.
Seals, dozing sleek on sliddery ledges
Slipt never, when by loftier edges
Through very inertia overthrown,
The impetuous ship in bafflement went down.

Hard Berg (methought), so cold, so vast,
With mortal damps self-overcast;
Exhaling still thy dankish breath—
Adrift dissolving, bound for death;
Though lumpish thou, a lumbering one—
A lumbering lubbard loitering slow,
Impingers rue thee and go down,
Sounding thy precipice below,
Nor stir the slimy slug that sprawls
Along thy dead indifference of walls.

Herman Melville

The City in the Sea

Lo! Death has reared himself a throne
In a strange city lying alone
Far down within the dim West,
Where the good and the bad and the worst and the best
Have gone to their eternal rest.
There shrines and palaces and towers
(Time-eaten towers that tremble not!)
Resemble nothing that is ours.
Around, by lifting winds forgot,
Resignedly beneath the sky
The melancholy waters lie.

No rays from the holy heaven come down
On the long night-time of that town;
But light from out the lurid sea
Streams up the turrets silently—
Gleams up the pinnacles far and free—
Up domes—up spires—up kingly halls—
Up fanes—up Babylon-like walls—
Up shadowy long-forgotten bowers
Of sculptured ivy and stone flowers—
Up many and many a marvelous shrine
Whose wreathéd friezes intertwine
The viol, the violet, and the vine.

Resignedly beneath the sky
The melancholy waters lie.
So blend the turrets and shadows there
That all seem pendulous in air,
While from a proud tower in the town
Death looks gigantically down.

There open fanes and gaping graves
Yawn level with the luminous waves;
But not the riches there that lie
In each idol's diamond eye—
Not the gaily-jeweled dead
Tempt the waters from their bed;
For no ripples curl, alas!
Along that wilderness of glass—
No swellings tell that winds may be
Upon some far-off happier sea—
No heavings hint that winds have been
On seas less hideously serene.

But lo, a stir is in the air!
The wave—there is a movement there!
As if the towers had thrust aside,
In slightly sinking, the dull tide—
As if their tops had feebly given
A void within the filmy Heaven.
The waves have now a redder glow—
The hours are breathing faint and low—
And when, amid no earthly moans,
Down, down that town shall settle hence,
Hell, rising from a thousand thrones,
Shall do it reverence.

Edgar Allan Poe

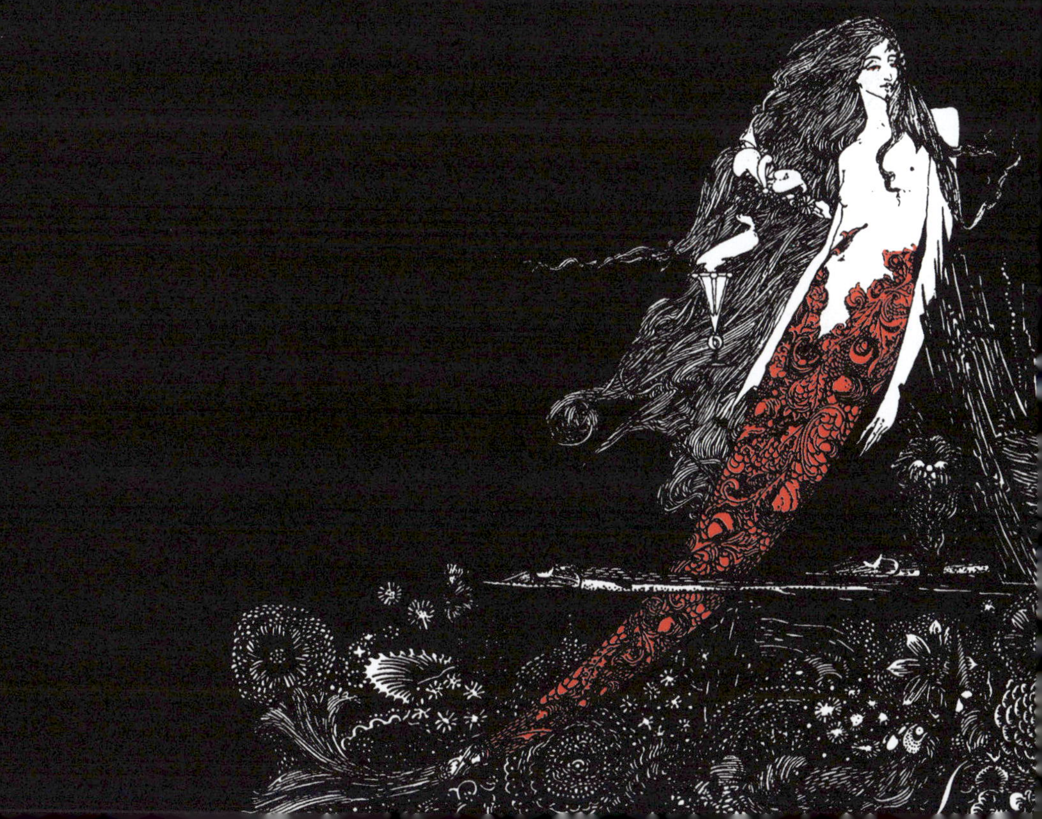

Full Fathom Five
(from *The Tempest*)

Full fathom five thy father lies;
Of his bones are coral made;
Those are pearls that were his eyes:
Nothing of him that doth fade,
But doth suffer a sea-change
Into something rich and strange.
Sea-nymphs hourly ring his knell:
D i n g - d o n g.
Hark! now I hear them—
Ding-dong, bell!

William Shakespeare

Hymn to Proserpine (extract)

All delicate days and pleasant, all spirits and sorrows are cast
Far out with the foam of the present that sweeps to the surf of the past:
Where beyond the extreme sea wall, and between the remote sea gates,
Waste water washes, and tall ships founder, and deep death waits:
Where, mighty with deepening sides, clad about with the seas as with wings,
And impelled of invisible tides, and fulfilled of unspeakable things,
White-eyed and poisonous-finned, shark-toothed and serpentinecurled,
Rolls, under the whitening wind of the future, the wave of the world.
The depths stand naked in sunder behind it, the storms flee away;
In the hollow before it the thunder is taken and snared as a prey;
In its sides is the north wind bound; and its salt is of all men's tears;
With light of ruin, and sound of changes, and pulse of years;
With travail of day after day, and with trouble of hour upon hour.
And bitter as blood is the spray; and the crests are as fangs that devour;
And its vapor and storm of its steam as the sighing of spirits to be;
And its noise as the noise in a dream; and its depth as the roots of the sea;
And the height of its heads as the height of the utmost stars of the air;
And the ends of the earth at the might thereof tremble, and time is made bare.
Will ye bridle the deep sea with reins, will ye chasten the high sea with rods?
Will ye take her to chain her with chains, who is older than all ye gods?
All ye as a wind shall go by, as a fire shall ye pass and be past;
Ye are gods, and behold, ye shall die, and the waves be upon you at last.
In the darkness of time, in the deeps of the years, in the changes of things,
Ye shall sleep as a slain man sleeps, and the world shall forget you or kings.

Algernon Charles Swinburne

The Ascent of Man (extract)

Sinking, swelling roared the wintry ocean,
    Pitch-black chasms struck with flying blaze,
As the cloud-winged storm-sky's sheer commotion
    Showed the blank Moon's mute Medusa face
White o'er wastes of water – surges crashing
    Over surges in the formless gloom,
And a mastless hulk, with great seas washing
    Her scourged flanks, pitched toppling to her doom.

Through the crash of wave on wave gigantic,
    Through the thunder of the hurricane,
My wild heart in breaking shrilled with frantic
    Exultation – 'Chaos come again!
Yea, let earth be split and cloven asunder
    With man's still accumulating curse –
Life is but a momentary blunder
    In the cycle of the Universe.'

Mathilde Blind

The Day of Judgement (extract)

When the fierce North-wind with his airy forces
Rears up the Baltic to a foaming fury;
And the red lightning with a storm of hail comes
Rushing amain down;

How the poor sailors stand amazed and tremble,
While the hoarse thunder, like a bloody trumpet,
Roars a loud onset to the gaping waters,
Quick to devour them.

Such shall the noise be and the wild disorder,
(If things eternal may be like these earthly),
Such the dire terror when the great Archangel
Shakes the creation;

Tears the strong pillars of the vault of Heaven,
Breaks up old marble, the repose of princes;
See the graves open, and the bones arising,
Flames all around them.

Hark, the shrill outcries of the guilty wretches!
Lively bright horror and amazing anguish
Stare through their eyelids, while the living worm lies
Gnawing within them.

Thoughts, like old vultures, prey upon their heart-strings,
And the smart twinges, when the eye beholds the
Lofty Judge frowning, and a flood of vengeance
Rolling afore him.

Hopeless immortals! how they scream and shiver,
While devils push them to the pit wide-yawning
Hideous and gloomy, to receive them headlong
Down to the centre!

Isaac Watts

And, the Last Day Being Come, Man Stood Alone

And, the last day being come, Man stood alone
Ere sunrise on the world's dismantled verge,
Awaiting how from everywhere should urge
The Coming of the Lord. And, behold, none

Did come,—but indistinct from every realm
Of earth and air and water, growing more
And louder, shriller, heavier, a roar
Up the dun atmosphere did overwhelm

His ears; and as he looked affrighted round
Every manner of beast innumerable
All thro' the shadows crying grew, until
The wailing was like grass upon the ground.

Asudden then within his human side
Their anguish, since the goad he wielded first,
And, since he gave them not to drink, their thirst,
Darted compressed and vital.—As he died,

Low in the East now lighting gorgeously
He saw the last sea-serpent iris-mailed
Which, with a spear transfixèd, yet availed
To pluck the sun down into the dead sea.

Trumbull Stickney

Vain Virtues (extract from *The House of Life*)

LXXXV

What is the sorriest thing that enters Hell?
    None of the sins, – but this and that fair deed
    Which a soul's sin at length could supersede.
These yet are virgins, whom death's timely knell
Might once have sainted; whom the fiends compel
    Together now, in snake-bound shuddering sheaves
    Of anguish, while the pit's pollution leaves
Their refuse maidenhood abominable.

Night sucks them down, the tribute of the pit,
    Whose names, half entered in the book of Life,
        Were God's desire at noon. And as their hair
And eyes sink last, the Torturer deigns no whit
    To gaze, but, yearning, waits his destined wife,
        The Sin still blithe on earth that sent them there.

Dante Gabriel Rossetti

Ulysses Describes His Visit to the Underworld
(extract from the *Odyssey*)

When to the powers beneath,
The sacred nation that survive with Death,
My prayers and vows had done devotions fit,
I took the offerings, and upon the pit
Bereft their lives. Out gushed the sable blood,
And round about me fled out of the flood
The souls of the deceased. There clustered then
Youths, and their wives, much suffering agèd men,
Soft tender virgins that but new came there
By timeless death, and green their sorrows were.
There men at arms, with armours all imbrued,
Wounded with lances and with falchions hewed,
In numbers up and down the ditch did stalk,
And threw unmeasured cries about their walk,
So horrid that a bloodless fear surprised
My daunted spirits.

Homer (trans. George Chapman)

The Pessimist's Vision

I dreamed, and saw a modern Hell, more dread
 Than Dante's pageant; not with gloom and glare,
 But all new forms of madness and despair
Filled it with complex tortures, some Earth-bred,
Some born in Hell: eternally full-fed
 Ghosts of all foul disease-germs thronged the air:
 And as with trembling feet I entered there,
A Demon barred the way, and mocking said –

'Through our dim vales and gulfs thou need'st not rove;
 From thine own Earth and from its happiest lot
  Thy lust for pain may draw full nourishment,
 With poignant spice of passion; knowest thou not
  Fiends wed for hate as mortals wed for love,
Yet find not much more anguish? Be content.'

Constance Naden

Darkness

I had a dream, which was not all a dream.
The bright sun was extinguish'd, and the stars
Did wander darkling in the eternal space,
Rayless, and pathless, and the icy earth
Swung blind and blackening in the moonless air;
Morn came, and went—and came, and brought no day,
And men forgot their passions in the dread
Of this their desolation; and all hearts
Were chill'd into a selfish prayer for light:
And they did live by watchfires—and the thrones,
The palaces of crowned kings—the huts,
The habitations of all things which dwell,
Were burnt for beacons; cities were consumed,
And men were gathered round their blazing homes
To look once more into each other's face;
Happy were those who dwelt within the eye
Of the volcanos, and their mountain-torch:
A fearful hope was all the world contain'd;
Forests were set on fire—but hour by hour
They fell and faded—and the crackling trunks
Extinguish'd with a crash—and all was black.
The brows of men by the despairing light
Wore an unearthly aspect, as by fits
The flashes fell upon them; some lay down
And hid their eyes and wept; and some did rest
Their chins upon their clenched hands, and smiled;
And others hurried to and fro, and fed
Their funeral piles with fuel, and looked up
With mad disquietude on the dull sky,
The pall of a past world; and then again
With curses cast them down upon the dust,
And gnash'd their teeth and howl'd: the wild birds shriek'd
And, terrified, did flutter on the ground,
And flap their useless wings; the wildest brutes
Came tame and tremulous; and vipers crawl'd
And twined themselves among the multitude,
Hissing, but stingless—they were slain for food:
And War, which for a moment was no more,
Did glut himself again;—a meal was bought
With blood, and each sate sullenly apart
Gorging himself in gloom: no love was left;

All earth was but one thought—and that was death
Immediate and inglorious; and the pang
Of famine fed upon all entrails—men
Died, and their bones were tombless as their flesh;
The meagre by the meagre were devoured,
Even dogs assail'd their masters, all save one,
And he was faithful to a corse, and kept
The birds and beasts and famish'd men at bay,
Till hunger clung them, or the dropping dead
Lured their lank jaws; himself sought out no food,
But with a piteous and perpetual moan,
And a quick desolate cry, licking the hand
Which answered not with a caress—he died.
The crowd was famish'd by degrees; but two
Of an enormous city did survive,
And they were enemies: they met beside
The dying embers of an altar-place,
Where had been heap'd a mass of holy things
For an unholy usage; they raked up,
And shivering scraped with their cold skeleton hands
The feeble ashes, and their feeble breath
Blew for a little life, and made a flame
Which was a mockery; then they lifted up
Their eyes as it grew lighter, and beheld
Each other's aspects—saw, and shriek'd, and died—
Even of their mutual hideousness they died,
Unknowing who he was upon whose brow
Famine had written Fiend. The world was void,
The populous and the powerful—was a lump,
Seasonless, herbless, treeless, manless, lifeless—
A lump of death—a chaos of hard clay.
The rivers, lakes, and ocean all stood still,
And nothing stirred within their silent depths;
Ships sailorless lay rotting on the sea,
And their masts fell down piecemeal; as they dropp'd
They slept on the abyss without a surge—
The waves were dead; the tides were in their grave,
The moon their mistress, had expired before;
The winds were withered in the stagnant air,
And the clouds perish'd; Darkness had no need
Of aid from them—She was the Universe.

George Gordon, Lord Byron

Index of Poems

Index of Poets

Credits

11: "The Furies" © Lavinia Singer, first published in *Falling Out of the Sky: Poems about Myths and Monsters* (The Emma Press, 2015). Reproduced by permission of the author. 12: "Outlaws" by Robert Graves (*The Complete Poems in One Volume*, eds. Beryl Graves and Dunstan Ward, 2000) is reprinted by permission of Carcanet Press on behalf of the Estate of Robert Graves. 13: Linda Hogan, "Skin" from *Dark. Sweet.: New & Selected Poems*. Copyright © 1993 by Linda Hogan. Reprinted with the permission of The Permissions Company, LLC on behalf of Coffee House Press, coffeehousepress.org. 14: "Worm Interviewed" by Ruthven Todd, reprinted by kind permission of Christopher Todd on behalf of the estate. 16–17: Kit Byford, "Appetit" from *He Said I Was a Peach* (ignitionpress, 2021). Copyright © Kit Byford, 2021. 19: Jeni Couzyn, "The Beast" from *Life By Drowning: Selected Poems* (Bloodaxe Books, 1985). Copyright © Jeni Couzyn, 1985. 32: "Do You Hear Me, Mere-Watcher" by *Laura Varnam, from Primers Volume Seven*, 2024 © Published by permission of Nine Arches Press. www.ninearchespress.com 35: Matt Goodfellow, "Ginny Greenteeth" from *Falling Out of the Sky* (Emma Press, 2015) Copyright © Matt Goodfellow, 2015. 40: Jo Brandon, "Wednesday's Child" from *Cures* (Valley Press, 2021). Copyright © Jo Brandon, 2021. 41: "Yuki Onna – Snow Woman" © Jan Dean, reproduced by permission of the author. 50 "The Name of the Father" by Laura Varnam, from *Primers Volume Seven*, 2024 © Published by permission of Nine Arches Press. www.ninearchespress.com 58: "Abduction" by Nuala Ní Dhomhnaill with translations into English by Michael Hartnett. By kind permission of the author and the translator's Estate c/o The Gallery Press, Loughcrew, Oldcastle, County Meath, Ireland, from *Selected Poems: Rogha Dánta* (1986, Raven Arts Press) 88: "Her Kind" by Anne Sexton, reprinted by permission of SLL/Sterling Lord Literistic, Inc. Copyright by Linda Gray Sexton. 90–91: "The Burning", copyright © Liz Berry 2020. 128: Bruce Boston, "Curse of the Strangler's Wife" from *Dark Matters* (Crossroad Press and Macabre Ink Digital, 2010). Bruce Boston was a major influential figure in speculative and genre poetry until his death in 2024. His poem is reproduced here with the permission of Marge Simon. 132: "each-uisge", copyright © Karan Chambers 2025, first published in *Gutter* Issue 29, 2024. 151: "The Morrigan Meets a Lover on the Battlefield" by Caroline Hardaker, from *Little Quakes Every Day* (Valley Press, 2021). By permission of the author. 156: "The Dancers" by Edith Sitwell reprinted by permission of Peters Fraser & Dunlop (www.petersfraserdunlop.com) on behalf of The Estate of Edith Sitwell. 172: "Following" by Eiléan Ní Chuilleanáin from *Collected Poems* (2020). By kind permission of the author and The Gallery Press, Loughcrew, Oldcastle, County Meath, Ireland. 173: Melissa Lee-Houghton, "Beautiful Girls" from *Beautiful Girls* (Penned in the Margins, 2013). Copyright © Melissa Lee-Houghton, 2013. 230: "The Execution" by Alden Nowlan from *Alden Nowlan Selected Poems* © 1996 House of Anansi Press. Reproduced with permission. www.houseofanansi.com 298: Angela Topping, "Earwig Country" from *Earwig Country* (Valley Press, 2024). Copyright © Angela Topping, 2024. 326: Rose Macaulay, "The Shadow", reproduced with the permission of The Society of Authors as the Literary Representative of the Estate of Rose Macaulay. 335: "Quicksand" by Nuala Ní Dhomhnaill with translations into English by Michael Hartnett. By kind permission of the author and the translator's Estate c/o The Gallery Press, Loughcrew, Oldcastle, County Meath, Ireland from *Selected Poems: Rogha Dánta* (1986, Raven Arts Press).

Cover illustration © Getty / duncan1890; pages 8, 19, 33, 43, 49, 53, 86, 93, 100, 111, 115, 123, 129, 133, 168, 173, 181, 183, 188, 193, 199, 226, 229, 242, 254, 275, 287, 293, 305, 309, 336, 347, 356 attributed to Harry Clarke (1889–1931); pages 22, 65 and 331 attributed to Joseph Jacobs (1854–1916); pages 21, 27, 119, 125, 134 and 167 courtesy of clipart.com.